CW01498048

Pitch Invasion

Pitch Invasion

My Story as a Feminist on a Football Club Board

Karen Dobres

CASSELL

First published in Great Britain in 2025 by Cassell, an imprint of
Octopus Publishing Group Ltd
Carmelite House
50 Victoria Embankment
London EC4Y 0DZ
www.octopusbooks.co.uk

An Hachette UK Company
www.hachette.co.uk

The authorized representative in the EEA is Hachette Ireland,
8 Castlecourt Centre, Dublin 15, D15 XTP3, Ireland (email: info@hbgi.ie)

Copyright © Karen Dobres 2025

Distributed in the US by Hachette Book Group
1290 Avenue of the Americas, 4th and 5th Floors
New York, NY 10104

Distributed in Canada by Canadian Manda Group
664 Annette St., Toronto, Ontario, Canada M6S 2C8

All rights reserved. No part of this work may be reproduced or utilized in any form or by any
means, electronic or mechanical, including photocopying, recording or by any information
storage and retrieval system, without the prior written permission of the publisher.

Karen Dobres asserts the moral right to be identified as the author of this work.

ISBN: 978-1-78840-588-1
eISBN: 978-1-78840-591-1

A CIP catalogue record for this book is available from the British Library.

Typeset in 11.5/18pt Plantin MT Pro by Six Red Marbles UK, Thetford, Norfolk

Printed and bound in Great Britain.

1 3 5 7 9 10 8 6 4 2

Publisher: Trevor Davies
Project Editor: Rimsha Falak
Copy Editor: Jane Selley
Creative Director: Mel Four
Designer: Clare Sivell
Production Controller: Sarah Parry
Picture Research Manager: Jennifer Veall

This FSC® label means that materials used for
the product have been responsibly sourced.

I'd like to dedicate this book to two intersecting communities of people.

One group is the women footballers who played in the past, alongside those who played on despite the ban, creating a history that was unearthed when 2017 allowed.

The other group consists of the thousands of volunteers and behind-the-scenes staff up and down the country who work tirelessly to keep women's and non-league men's club football running. Since parachuting into the 'Football Family' from an alien land, I have been repeatedly struck by the dedication and hard work of the many, many people who keep their clubs going. I mean those who work for nothing or for very little recompense to get the shows on the road. Before I worked at Lewes FC my impression of 'football' came from the front and back pages of newspapers, externally facing accounts of the game's extremes, from pictures of male players lounging in jacuzzies and reports of them assaulting women, to hooligans rampaging around the world, and a lot of fuss and column inches over 'big matches'. Now I have a very different understanding of the meaning and purpose of football and believe that the community behind it is extraordinary – largely unrewarded, passionate and united in a way that world leaders can only dream of. And, to the board, staff and volunteers of Lewes FC in particular – my wish is that every fan could see and appreciate the countless hours of unseen work you do.

– Karen Dobres, February 2025

Contents

Introduction
I Don't Like Football

────

The game of football is quite unsuitable for
women and ought not to be encouraged.

The FA, 1921

It's 1994. I'm at Wembley Stadium watching England v USA. It's boring and I hate being here. We're sitting high up on a tiered row. The fold-down seats are hard, the floor is steel grey – concrete, sticky. Men hold plastic pints of beer while shouting at the pitch. The crowd are clearly passionate about whatever is going on down there, and all around me deep voices rise and fall as one. To a man (I see no women here) they know what they think, and why they think it. I haven't a clue what that might be, and why it seems so important. I'm lost and out of place.

As a rule of thumb, I choose not to be near men who have consumed alcohol and are angry or worked up in any way, so I'm feeling slightly threatened. Also, I'm repelled by everything life has taught me thus far about the game of football. Hooligan fans, over-rewarded male egos who hang out in jacuzzis, and taking over the front AND back of newspapers that I otherwise want to read. As for any appeal to women, that seems to be confined to the WAGs, who are made fun of and endlessly papped for no reason other than that they are, quite literally, wives and girlfriends, existing only in relation to the real protagonists. I don't question that it's the world's most popular sport, with some 3.6 billion fans around the globe. But those fans are mostly blokes, or blokes-in-training, and seem to see something of themselves reflected in the sport. They also know the rules of the game, the norms of the terraces, and random facts about cups, matches, teams, players and things called 'Christmas tree formations'. I know, and want to know, nothing about any of these.

A boyfriend brought me here today. He said he had tickets for an 'exciting event at Wembley'. I'd rushed out of my counselling college in Ealing to meet him at Wembley Park Tube station, thinking we were off to see Take That. I was very disappointed to find that in fact we were joining this beery throng of England supporters to watch sweaty men for an hour and a half. Talk about him not reading the room! I am gutted. This is emphatically *not* my kind of date.

★ ★ ★

It's 2018. I'm back at Wembley for the second time after a 29-year gap. This time I'm in a smart and spacious meeting room – a 'corporate box' – off a long corridor leading to many similar meeting rooms, all proffering luxury biscuits atop huge, shiny circular tables, and imposing views of the football pitch. This time I'm a vital part of a six-strong consortium pitching to the top brass of the Women's FA for an obscure team called Lewes FC Women to go into the Championship – the second-highest league of English women's football – following a restructuring of the women's game. There are no fewer than seven people from the FA sitting in front of us, resplendent in suits, blouses and ties. The surroundings are grand, the people polite and the atmosphere formal. And I'm gazing through a massive window overlooking that world-famous ground, despite the undisputed fact that I lack knowledge of the game itself, and wouldn't have recognised Ronaldo, Messi or Pele if I'd bumped into them in one of the many corridors we've walked through to get here.

So how did this happen? How did I, a trained counselling professional, former catwalk model and avowed football outsider find myself a director on the board of a football club? How did I go from disliking and actively avoiding the so-called beautiful game to playing a part in getting Lewes into the Championship and becoming one of the architects of its pioneering gender equality campaign? And how did I end up – again, despite not knowing the offside rule or who won which cup when – being a key figure in the club's successful search for 'unwelcome women' fans and fair-minded folk to supply proof of concept for a brilliant and risky levelling of the playing field, and then leading on Lewes FC's groundbreaking 'Impact on the World' strategy?

Chapter 1
A Town of Radicals

We have it in our power to build the world anew.

Thomas Paine

We moved from London to Lewes in 2007 – we being me (Karen), my husband, Charlie, the man who took me on that disappointing football date, and our two small children. Charlie and I didn't know the town very well, but there was a small alternative school there, where we hoped the kids would thrive.

That should have been the first clue as to the nature of Lewes. The former county town of East Sussex is home to a castle, a prison, a police HQ, the county courts, the oldest outdoor swimming pool in England, the ruins of a medieval Cluniac priory, an extensive network of twittens (alleyways), 17,000 people, a football club, the biggest bonfire celebration in the country, and various ley lines – mystical direct pathways between ancient monuments along which energy is said to travel.

Lewes New School, down in the Pells area of town, was started by a small group of activist parents and educators who were doing things differently from the mainstream. It allowed kids to learn at their own pace and through their own curiosity, and the curriculum was co-created by kids and teachers, and sometimes parents. As a person-centred counsellor by profession, I was keen on the 'respectful communication' model promoted by the school. I liked the fact that kids addressed staff by their first names so that the power was shared more equally, and loved the slightly rebellious nature of nearly everybody I met there. 'If we get a good Ofsted report,' one parent told me, 'then we know we're doing something wrong.' The truth was that the parents and teachers who originally set up the school had opted for their own set of 'special measures' some years ago. In our first week of waiting in the playground at home time, one child proudly told me, 'This school lets me be myself.' I was quickly sold.

I remember our son's first lessons in Reception fondly. If it wasn't teddy bears' picnics in the woods, where den-making was the objective, it was growing green tomatoes, making chutney, then selling it with his classmates and teachers after school. The kids had to learn counting, planting, caring, harvesting, domestic science, writing, plant biology and business to make that chutney – the project ended up taking two terms, and they were absolutely fired up for it. Having helped out at our daughter's primary school in London, where overworked teachers were effectively herding cats from classroom to playground while following a system that did its best to squeeze the joy out of learning, I wasn't about to disagree with the thinking at Lewes New School. And its small size meant my kids wouldn't be lost within a bigger system, and everyone would know each other personally. That felt human and safe to me. There was a problem when Glastonbury was on, of course, because half the teaching staff and kids were absent, and you couldn't throw a herbal tea bag in the playground without hitting a poet or a shaman, but we managed well, with the children flourishing for the most part, and I enjoyed being an involved parent governor there.

We weren't long into our first term when 5 November came around. We'd been warned about Lewes Bonfire, 'the most famous in the UK' ('What? But there are only 17,000 residents in this town – how can it be?'), but nothing could have prepared us for the ambition and dogged rebellion of the citizens of Lewes, who proudly marched with the town's bonfire societies, or the spectacularly skilful hand-crafted tableaux effigies, or the scale of the fantastic firework displays with their six simultaneous grand finales. Shockingly (but what a laugh!), bangers are sometimes placed in the town's parking meters, because 'Why should we make the parking authorities rich?' If you haven't been to Lewes Bonfire (and I'm guessing you haven't, because, believe me, the town doesn't make it easy, closing all transport links early on and saying it's only for Lewesians), it's spectacular, dark, and barrel-rollingly outrageous.

In theory, Bonfire commemorates – among other acts of rebellion – the 17 Protestant martyrs imprisoned and burned at the stake in Lewes between 1555 and 1557. Hike up the sloping downs from the old Cliffe area and you will pass an obelisk engraved with their names. From here, if you look in a straight line to the centre of town, you will see the Angel statue, remembering those Lewesians who gave their lives fighting for our country. Another ley line.

This is a town that wears its history on its sleeve. Every cobbled street, shady twitten and bend of the River Ouse, which winds through it, would tell a story if only it could speak. A little further along the river, in Rodmell, Virginia Woolf's body was found one day in April 1941 by a small gang of boys. One of them, Norman Ashcroft, now in his nineties, also arranged fundraising concerts for the local football club at Lewes Town Hall back in the late sixties, and Pink Floyd were happy to play to help pay for new floodlights at Lewes FC's ground, the Dripping Pan.[1]

I knew it wouldn't be long before I came to the Dripping Pan, that cauldron of dreams with the bewitching name, set in the South Downs National Park, its old flint walls edging the hollowed-out football pitch that is its core. Home to Lewes Football Club – the mighty Rooks. Our ground, our fortress.

Lewes FC was formed in 1885, when members of the cricket club that played there wanted something to do in the winter. They founded the football club in the upstairs room of the Royal Oak pub in Station Street on 23 September of that year, and football has been played at the Dripping Pan ever since. People often ask

---

1   There's another Pink Floyd connection to come later in this story.

how the ground got its Harry Potteresque name. Well, legend has it that the Cluniac monks in the nearby (now tenderly preserved) Priory Ruins used to pan for salt in the surrounding marshy land, and their pans would drip with water while retaining the valuable salt.

Another thing about those monks – they looked after the captured King Henry III, 'much beaten with swords and maces', when he was defeated by barons led by Simon de Montfort at the Battle of Lewes in 1264. The barons disagreed with the Divine Right of Kings and effectively established the first parliamentary democracy in Lewes, ruling the country independently of the king for some months afterward. That was so Lewes.

It's clear from the above that a drive towards a fairer existence for all is written into the fabric of our town. Thomas Paine – political activist and one of the Founding Fathers of American democracy – famously lived here from 1768 to 1774. In many respects, Lewes is where Paine was, to put it in modern parlance, 'radicalised'. While shacked up in the high street there, he wrote an influential tome condemning corruption within the customs and excise service, and developed some of the ideas that ultimately led to American independence. Nowadays a pub called Rights of Man stands nearby, named after his most famous book, in which the rebel Paine defended the revolution in France, arguing that a nation should be able to choose its government, and that government itself should exist and function to protect human rights. He then rejected Christianity and moved to America. Lewes is so proud of

Paine's long stay that there is a statue of him outside the town's library.

By now you get the picture about this vocal, upstart town. Lewes has a knack for attracting fans of change! Bringing us nicely back to Lewes FC and those who support it.

Chapter 2
Equality FC

It is justice, not charity, that is wanting in the world.

Mary Wollstonecraft

Husband Charlie has always been a football fan. Born and bred in Southend, he was a proud Southend United season ticket holder when we met, and our family Hurt Museum[2] displays the sorry tale of my labour with our first child. We were living in Kilburn, north-west London, at the time, and I went into labour two weeks late. That's right, it was an 'any time now' situation. Despite this

2   'Hurt Museum' is a term I learned during my counselling training from one of my excellent trainers, who had a sense of humour. It refers to an imaginary space in one's psyche where memories of suffering are stored and occasionally brought out – like exhibits – to be examined and discussed (often at the expense of whoever caused the hurt in question – in this case, Charlie). Perhaps you have a Hurt Museum too? Hours of fun. The same trainer also taught me the Freudian-sounding phrase 'If it's not one thing, it's your mother'. A handy mnemonic for any aspiring therapist, or therapee, for that matter.

fact, a kind neighbour ended up taking me to hospital because Charlie was, of course, two hours' drive away at Roots Hall football stadium, watching Southend. There are similar tales in the same museum involving football as an unworthy priority. So when we moved to Lewes, it was no surprise to me that he started to go and watch his new local team play.

Lewes FC is nicknamed 'the Rooks' for two reasons: the abundance of grey-beaked black corvids that nest around the Dripping Pan, cleaning up leftover chips after a game; and the town's statement Norman castle on the hill. Both emblems are neatly represented on the club badge, and in the fans' songs, the most popular at the time being a ditty to the tune of 'When the Saints Go Marching In' celebrating the birds' messy effect on visitors' cars (that one lives grimly on to this day, its jubilant nature always raising smiles). Personally, though, I took little interest in Charlie's fandom at first, just enjoying his enthusiasm when the men's non-league team won, and the occasional tale of Cynical Dave said this, Gary the Badge was on good form, Big Deaksy did that, etc.

Two years later, in 2009, the global financial crisis hit. Privately owned Lewes FC faced financial ruin, and fans were concerned about its future. A contact at school introduced Charlie to the then local writer and football fan Patrick Marber, to see if between the two of them they could somehow find a way forward for the club. In December 2009, Charlie and I were invited to a dinner party where we met Ed Ramsden, investment manager and born-and-bred Lewesian. Charlie and Ed talked about Lewes FC all night, both interested in finding a way to save the club from impending financial ruin, using Ed's financial knowledge and Charlie's marketing and business expertise. They both look back on that night as 'the most expensive dinner party we ever went to'.

By 2010, Ed, Charlie and Patrick had hooked up with three other fans – Alex Leith, Ben Ward and Nick Williams – all living locally, passionate about Lewes FC and bringing their own skills to the table. These 6 men, calling themselves 'Rooks 125' (because 2010 marked 125 years since the club's foundation), bought the club for a nominal pound, paid off its debts and, after months of legal, financial, governance and social communications, transferred it from private to fan ownership. On 8 July 2010, Lewes FC became a mass-owned 'community benefit society', with the six men forming the inaugural executive board, working as volunteers to install working practices and procedures during the season before opening to wider community ownership in 2011.

I remember long discussions, phone calls, meetings, negotiations, and the passion of the group for this model of football ownership. I couldn't help being touched by the story of the men's team manager, Steve Ibbotson ('Ibbo'), needing to retire, but still managing to pay the players' wages from his own pension money. Even though I didn't like football, I bought a single share and became an owner of Lewes FC to support this idea of social ownership and the new direction the club was taking. I was also impressed that celebrity friends of Patrick's, such as Nigella Lawson and Jo Brand, were becoming owners alongside lots of local fans. Ownership was open to everyone, and my £30 share got me a badge, a certificate, and a vote at the annual elections as to who should be on the board. It also meant I was eligible to stand for the board myself should I want – something I'd never have dreamed of at the time, having neither interest in nor knowledge of football. My focus lay elsewhere, and I was more than content to keep things that way.

In 2016, however, Charlie – having looked thoughtful for some weeks now – casually asked me what would turn out to be a fateful question: 'What would you say if the club decided it was going to pay the women's team the same as the men's?'

I looked at him incredulously, my brain starting to buzz. Instead of a straight answer, I fired two questions back: 'What? Wait. There are *women* there playing football?', closely followed by: 'There are women playing football and they *don't* get paid the same as the men?!'

What followed was an hour's session on 'Sexism in Football', and then another on 'The Impact on the World of Sexism in Football'.

I learned that despite once achieving bigger crowds than men at their matches, women had been banned by the FA from playing football for a period of 50 years. In a shameful move on 5 December 1921, the Football Association had held a meeting in London at which they announced an outright ban on women playing on FA-affiliated pitches, stating that 'The game of football is quite unsuitable for females and ought not to be encouraged.' In one fell swoop, they effectively destroyed football for women and rendered it a male domain, in which female players were lucky to get crumbs from the table of the men's team at any club at which they were 'allowed' to play.

It took mere seconds for a very heavy penny to drop and for me to realise that this ban was why I hadn't known that women and football were a thing. When I dwelled on it for a minute, I realised that I'd basically (unconsciously) assumed that women just weren't *good* at football. The fact that we weren't good at it had been no problem in my mind, of course, because everything about the football I had been exposed to seemed either threatening, boring or unappealing. And yet, with just that teensy bit of knowledge about the history of women's football in this country, I began to see my primary school playground in a different light. The ban had only been lifted in 1971 and I was at primary school in the seventies – no wonder it had been only the boys who'd played it! And again, no wonder there had only been netball on offer when I got to senior school. We girls had been prevented from playing football by the knock-on effects of the ban.

In that moment, I felt angry for having been deliberately excluded from the world's most popular sport. And angry that the football club of which I was an owner didn't currently pay the women who played there the same as the men. (These were pioneering women, surely, breaking from the norm and following their passion. They needed support!) I also felt ashamed of my own lack of imagination – why hadn't I even considered that women played football? Why had I assumed that they (read 'we') weren't good at it? When Charlie divulged that the women's game drew only a quarter of the fans that the men got, I immediately resolved to go and watch a women's football match at the Dripping Pan. I'd change that sorry statistic by one, I decided, and expand my horizon at the same time.

For context, at this point in my life I was bringing up a teenage girl and a boy who'd just left primary school. I was concerned about what I saw as a backward trend in feminism. It seemed to me that the girls I knew from my daughter's circles were opinionated and thoughtful in private spaces and at home, but once they were on a public platform – like Instagram – they often postured to make themselves look good, and seemed happy to follow trends and objectify themselves. I know I can sound like a right old crusty, but I wanted better for my kids and the kids I knew. I'm also aware that for some years of my life I'd personally profited from fashion modelling, where I'd objectified myself to sell clothes (though I'd been clear about why I was doing what I was doing and the transactional nature of it), but I truly felt that what these teenagers were being exposed to was more insidious, and worse for their mental health. It seemed that social media could blur the line between fiction and reality, between image and self. Up until now, though, I'd felt there was little anyone could do to change this culture.

The following Sunday, I walked the short distance from my home to the Dripping Pan, feeling both a little unsure and a little weird. Although many men I knew did this a lot, it was the first time for me. I was going out, on my own, to watch a football match – I felt like a social experiment.

I got there 15 minutes before kick-off and there was no crowd at all, just a friendly face at the turnstile as I paid for my ticket. In I walked to see just a handful of people dotted around the 2,500-capacity stadium. No rowdy groups of men, and nobody batted an eye that I was here alone. In fact, there was a distinct and refreshing atmosphere of *not* being looked at, not being judged; just being there to watch the pitch, where players from the two teams were stretching, running, and generally being put through their paces by guys in dark tracksuits. I'd find out soon enough that they were the coaches, and that this unselfconscious display was the official warm-up. There was pop music playing. I was out of place, but relaxed.

After getting a cup of tea from a hatch at the clubhouse (the Rook Inn, of course) I went to stand by the old flint wall on the north side of the ground, because that was where the afternoon sunshine was falling. All I really knew was that the match would last for 90 minutes, with a break for half-time. I didn't even know that half-time was 15 minutes long – just like an interval at the theatre – but again, I'd find out soon enough. Ignorant of the rules of football itself, and the cultural norms of fans in the terraces, I was nonetheless happy to be there in my own way and simply observe. It all seemed surprisingly peaceful and unthreatening. As the game kicked off, I found myself standing, cuppa in hand, with a woman on my left and a man on my right, both happy to share their observations on the action down on the pitch. The crowd was fairly quiet except when a goal was scored, or likely to be scored, and everyone was unobtrusively amicable. It was a far cry from what I'd seen of your average stadium atmosphere on the telly (which had, of course, been exclusively men's matches).

But I need to tell you about the female players, because watching them I had a kind of epiphany. They were out there in public, giving their all to the game and each other. To a woman they were focused, determined, powerful, aggressive and not in the least afraid of falling over and getting back up. During those 90 minutes, I witnessed displays of resilience, decision-making ability, teamwork and young women not caring what they looked like. To me this was remarkable. These women were free, and you know one thing they definitely were not? Ornaments. After about 20 minutes, I found I was smiling. By half-time, I realised that I felt stronger vicariously just by watching them play. I was convinced this wouldn't be the case had I been watching men. These women could have been me. Admittedly, at a massive stretch, but the point is: they were *women*!

They were all aged probably between about 18 and 35, but that didn't stop me, aged 49, seeing myself right there reflected on the pitch. I felt each blow, and could imagine myself making that save or taking that corner – scenarios that had never occurred to me when I'd seen men play on the TV. I wanted to bring my daughter and her friends along, so that they could share in this inspiration. And my son, so that he could see this brilliant version of womanhood. And all my friends, so that they could be buoyed up just like I was. Where else had I seen women being free and strong like this in public? Nowhere. I decided right then, on the spot, that this was the antidote to the sexist guff we all had to live with every day in the media. Women's football was the stereotype-bashing phenomenon that we all needed more of. I was loving it. And yet . . . only a hundred or so people watching? What was going wrong here?

Ed and Charlie thought they knew, and that by insisting on not only paying Lewes FC Women the same as Lewes FC Men, but also giving them equal marketing resources, they could change the status quo and set an example to the rest of football and beyond. Having got over my initial shock – at the criminal under-resourcing of female players, the fact they'd previously been banned from playing by their own federation, and the way all this was either unknown or normalised – I was inspired by these two men. They had decided to see the water in which they, and football itself, were swimming, and insist on change. On the board they had questioned the fairness of giving the Step 7[3] men's team (ten times) more budget than the Step 3[4] women's, when the women were clearly doing well and sacrificing so much time and energy to play for Lewes. They had resolved to increase the playing budget for the women to the same level as the men for the following season. And ultimately this was from their own pockets, so that the men's team would not lose out in any way.

3   A Step 7 men's football team plays at the seventh level of the English league system. This falls under 'non-league football', which sits below the professional leagues but remains highly competitive.

4   A Step 3 women's team competes in the third tier of the women's football pyramid, just below the two professional leagues. It likely includes a mix of amateur and semi-professional players. As a result, players often have other jobs alongside football.

As the board of directors were not unanimous on making such a drastic change, Charlie and Ed proposed to stand for re-election on the basis that they would bring in 'Equality FC',[5] equalising budgets. They both passionately believed that resourcing the women would not only be the right thing to do, but also bring in more sponsors and owners, and, crucially, raise that low gate figure for the women. In other words, it was right both morally and commercially.

As for me, I walked home that sunny Sunday that bit taller, that bit more fired up than I had been before. I thought about why I was a feminist in the first place. I'd always hated the unfairness of the fact that being a woman meant I had fewer rights and privileges than men. As I passed the Royal Oak with its blue plaque proudly stating that 'Lewes FC was formed here in 1885', I reflected that a specific part of my life experience had, up to this point, been curtailed. I had never known about these women because football had been owned by men. And yet women's football is empowering – it's visceral, I could feel it. Looking back, I'd say I had some kind of 'aha moment' – as they say in therapy – at the Dripping Pan that day, and subsequently my life was about to change.

As for Charlie and Ed, they wrote their election addresses making it clear that if elected they would press for equal budgets for both first teams. Why? Because they were proud feminists and

5   The name of the groundbreaking campaign by which Lewes FC became the first pro or semi-pro club in the world to equalise playing budgets between male and female players.

believed it was the right thing to do. Ed's speech was eloquent, drawing on American novelist David Foster Wallace's famous fish story: 'There are these two young fish swimming along, and they happen to meet an older fish swimming the other way, who nods at them and says, "Morning boys, how's the water?" And the two young fish swim on for a bit, and then eventually one of them looks over at the other and goes, "What the hell is water?"' Ed went on to explain with current examples. He described how men's football had become the water we were all swimming in, insisting that it had become synonymous with football itself. No one questioned this or thought about it, just as fish don't question the water they swim in. Men's football was so normalised – so uncontested as the definition of the game – that it was the sole reference for the word 'football'. He noted how sparse the media reporting on women's matches was. Pointing out a current newspaper headline promising 'All the action from the weekend' but reporting exclusively on men's matches, he lamented, 'You would have thought no women's matches had been played, even though many had, up and down the country.' The BBC football website alone boasted 33 features on a snapshot day in September 2016 – all of them men's. He pointed out that 99.6 per cent of sports sponsorship money went to men's sport and 0.4 per cent to women's. He ended with a mic drop, 'Try explaining to a child, girl or boy, why it's OK for less than one penny of every pound to be spent on females. I mean it. Try it. This is water.'

Every owner of Lewes FC was sent the election addresses to read, as usual, prior to exercising our votes. To my mind, it was powerful stuff. How dare the establishment stop women from playing and consuming the world's most popular sport? How dare they stop us developing the hopes and dreams that boys and men had always had? How dare they take football away from us and conspire to make us think that was normal, that that was OK, that it was what we all wanted?

Sure enough, both men were re-elected for the following season, and on 8 July 2017, gender equality was introduced to one of the most male of male bastions, football. By little Lewes FC.

Chapter 3
Made in Neasden

———

We're on the way to Wembley . . . You have to go through
Neasden to get there.

Private Eye cartoon

I think that once I understood the word, I realised I'd always
considered myself a feminist. As Maya Angelou said, 'I'd be
stupid not to be on my own side.' I remember how the pictures
of topless women in the copies of the *Sun* and the *Mirror* we had
around the house in Neasden, where I was born and bred, made
me feel uncomfortable. My dad's frequent sexist comments about
women's bodies were designed, he said, to make me and my sister
'unshockable'. They probably did have that effect, bless him, but
they also gave me a way to relate to the patriarchal subjugation
of women – to see it all as a bit of a joke designed for men; to
disassociate and rise above it.

Which is exactly what I did in regard to the game of football.
At primary school, football was for the boys, who took up most

of the playground playing it. This claim to space was accepted without question, and we girls were relegated to the edges, for hopscotch and chatting. At the time this felt completely normal – we simply shrugged our shoulders if the boys bumped into us, or if we felt crowded. But now, with my modern lens, I can perceive it as a nod to both boys and girls about who is entitled to more space when genders are grouped together. Those boys were being trained to spread their trousered legs on a Tube train later in life. We were being trained to cross ours and make ourselves smaller.

By the time I went to senior school – John Kelly Girls, the local state school, in the same road as our house – this experience was eliminated. And, needless to say, we didn't play football because it wasn't on offer. The boys' equivalent (John Kelly Boys) was right next door, and we shared both an entrance and a Marmite reputation. Some people raved about the girls' school, and for religious reasons the sex segregation was a deliberate choice for the families of many girls who travelled in on public transport from across the London Borough of Brent, from areas like Harlesden, Colindale, Wembley and Kilburn. However, there were often fights outside the school gates, and the police visited on and off over the years to deal with various violent incidents, mainly from the boys, but sometimes from the harder girls too. At our school, 'hard' meant scary. It was a compliment – 'she's well 'ard' denoted high status, but someone to approach with some caution all the same. I was not 'well 'ard'. I was studious, friendly and nicknamed 'Lanky' by my friends, due to the fact that I was tall and gangly.

John Kelly School has gone through several incarnations since I was there, becoming an academy which is no longer single sex. Googling it recently, I find a comment from a few years back stating that it's a 'poor secondary school' where 'kids are violent'. I might have *partially* agreed with *half* of this statement but it feels reductive because the girls' school was much more than some kind of fight club, at least when I attended. I remember caring teachers inviting us into their own homes during O levels, when teachers' strikes threatened our ability to cover the syllabus. An engaged student, I enjoyed working – knowing myself to be competent at reading and writing, and at seeing both sides of an argument while pushing one forward. I liked the academic aspect of school, and as I grew older, I also enjoyed the social life – visiting the new Brent Cross Shopping Centre (I loved my part-time sales job in Ravel shoe shop and being able to get discounted shoes and bags for friends and family) and the Production Village pub in nearby Cricklewood with schoolmates. Cut in half by the North Circular Road, Neasden didn't exactly have a thriving social scene, unless you count a shared banana split at the Wimpy in the shopping centre off the massive roundabout, or hanging out by the swings in Gladstone Park on Dollis Hill Lane. Famously, *Private Eye* magazine satirised the place as a recurring joke, using it to 'denote the contemporary urban environment' of parts of outer London. They even gave it an unsuccessful fictional football team: Neasden FC.

Our school's resources were limited, as I've since found out with the benefit of comparison to others. For example, I was disappointed not to be able to choose geography at A level because John Kelly wasn't able to offer it. We were at an advantage, though, when it came to diversity. I keenly attended, and reported back to school on, the anti-racism conferences organised by our local MP, Ken Livingstone. (I still have *Rock Against Racism* stickers on saved youthful diaries from gigs we travelled to in central London as teenagers.) Racism was very relevant to our lives at that time, as our school's catchment area was multi-ethnic, and I noticed from my early teens how my brown and black friends were treated differently from me outside of school, on the buses, in the shops. Not for them the unquestioned free social pass that white people seemed to enjoy in our country. I remember an enlightening conversation I had with one of my (black) friends at school that has always stuck in my mind and has been practically and emotionally useful ever since. Around 1984 – five years before the term 'intersectionality' was coined by Kimberlé Williams Crenshaw – my friend told me that during my life if I ever needed a surgeon or a lawyer, I should try my hardest to find a black woman for the job. When I asked her why, she sighed that a black woman would have had to be smarter and better at overcoming obstacles than anyone else in the profession – she'd have an expertise you could count on when you really needed it. My experiences as a teenager with my schoolfriends meant that I understood and believed what she was saying.

At school, I loved English literature, languages, geography, and playing in the steel band. While my modern comprehensive might have made me streetwise and able to relate to a variety of people, it didn't, at the time, give me the ambition to go to university. There simply wasn't the expectation. Not many from our school generally applied, and both my parents had left school at fourteen without qualifications.

After A levels, I went off to Germany with my friend Odette (we'd studied German together), where we shared a large room in a *Wohngemeinschaft* (communal flat) in Frankfurt, living with five other people, all in their thirties and paid-up members of Die Grünen (the Green Party). Our German was just about good enough for us to get jobs as waitresses in a restaurant, at a time when there were still American GIs in Frankfurt and the Berlin Wall still separated the East from the West. Surprisingly for us, coming as we did from Neasden, Odette was one of very few black women in Frankfurt at that time, and the American GIs – who all seemed to be young black men – were obsessed with her British accent. They'd never heard a black woman speak like that ('apart from Sade'), and kept asking her to say something, just to marvel in delight at this Britishness flowing so freely from her mouth. We became regulars at the Funkadelic nightclub on a Thursday night, making American friends there and walking home together for safety.

After a couple of months scouring the jobs pages of the *Frankfurter Allgemeine Zeitung*, we found better-paid work in commercial organisations, and, confidence no doubt increased by this independent adventure in another country, encouraged each other to apply for UK university places. In the meantime, we were living near the city's red-light district, on the Kaiserstrasse, enduring salubrious comments from random men on our way to and from home. 'Baby, baby, come with me' and 'What you doing tonight, baby?' were constant and boring refrains. They were creepy invasions of personal space, and yet they were completely unremarkable. My parents had always told me to take positive public comments from men about my appearance as flattering and walk on. I tried to, but, in reality, I rarely regarded these interruptions as compliments, as there was an undercurrent of threat attached to them. And yet *everyone* accepted them, and so did Odette and I. Being catcalled and spoken to salaciously by male strangers on the street was just part of the social wallpaper for young women as I was growing up (and would be until Laura Bates called it out some twenty-six years later with her #EverydaySexism campaign).

After my stint as a waitress (the pressure of taking orders in another language was *real*; I have endless patience with foreign waiting staff to this day), I got a job with a Japanese pharmaceutical company as a scientific editor, making sure that reports of clinical trials were in good English for the British Department of Health and Social Security and the US Food and Drug Administration. One morning, Mr Yokoyama, our CEO, spread out a map of London across my desk and asked where Turnham Green was. I racked my brain, edged my finger west and, by some fluke, pointed it out. 'Ah, good,' he said. 'Because you are from London, you will buy us an office.' So it happened that at just eighteen years old, I was tasked with finding a large 'London liaison office' with easy access to Heathrow for one of the largest pharmaceutical companies in Japan. My friends were impressed when I was flown business class back and forth from Frankfurt, taking black taxis everywhere and carrying huge amounts of cash in a suitcase. I was once asked to buy a British Racing Green Rolls-Royce, and paid for it with fresh, crisp fifty-pound notes, much to the surprise of the west London dealership.

The company rewarded my efforts by sponsoring me through university – English literature at Bristol – where I was able to buy and run a second-hand yellow VW Beetle, with the security of 12 weeks' paid work every summer in London or Frankfurt. I was amazed at the opulence of the university, with its Olympic-sized swimming pool in the student union, and all kinds of societies to join. By contrast, my boyfriend, who had been to Eton, was distinctly *un*impressed, declaring the pool 'a bit scummy'. He'd never been to Granville Road public baths in Kilburn, though, had he?

I learned karate while at university, and got to grips with studying Anglo-Saxon for my degree, enjoying the quirkiness of tutorials where the 'Old English' cohort would have a glass of sherry with our professor. We were all wildly impressed that Professor Burrow understood Elvish, having been taught by the great Tolkien himself at Oxford. For a while I became treasurer of the Afro-Caribbean Society – partly because they were so short of members (there really weren't many black students at Bristol University in those days) and partly because I felt most at home within a multicultural setting.

While at Bristol, I co-edited, produced and wrote for a free student magazine, deciding I wanted to be a journalist. However, in my final year, while I was modelling at a student fashion show at a nightclub, a young woman tapped me on the shoulder to ask if I'd come to London to model with her agency, Elite Models. With absolutely zero plans in place for my journalistic career, but intending to move back to my home city anyway, and aware that I'd need money to pay rent, I agreed to go for test shots. The people at the agency seemed nice enough, but the profession was precarious, and before anyone could judge my shots too harshly, I decided to join my then boyfriend, who was off to live and work in Key West, Florida, for a while. There I got a casual job selling glass-bottom boat ride tickets (the coral reef was stunning) and acting as a kayak guide through the mangroves when my employer had German tourists. I also met a hypnotist and past life therapist, who chose me as a mentee. Weekends were spent either at her past life regression classes or swotting up on the flora and fauna of the mangroves and translating the information into German. I learned about Ernest Hemingway, who had lived on the island, bought my first pair of Birkenstocks, celebrated the sunset with the rest of the islanders every night, delved into hypnosis, and was grateful for the exciting time spent there.

On our return to the UK seven months later, however, my boyfriend and I split up. Once again jobless, I went back to the model agency. 'Sorry,' they said, 'we've got someone who looks like you now.' They seemed pretty piqued that I'd left without warning (I hadn't taken the idea of modelling very seriously back then). Incomeless, and with no better plan at that time, I visited another agency, Options in Baker Street, and was sent for more tests. When the shots came back, my booker, Nigel, called me in and told me I'd be doing a Zandra Rhodes show the next day. Nervous, but used to winging it by now, I was grateful (and a little surprised!) when he whipped out a pair of red heels from behind his desk to teach me how to catwalk. He was magnificent as he strutted across the office, giving me my first (and only) modelling lesson. According to him, all I needed to do was put one foot in front of the other, turn without falling over, and guard against a hand on one hip and an arm out on the other side – 'It's strictly no teapots, darling!' He worked the room like a pro, exuding attitude. On his very strict orders, I rushed out to buy 'essentials' – size 7 black heels and a nude thong – and went to bed early.

The show went well. At least I didn't fall over, sweat my make-up off or smile too much. And I was grateful to be rebooked. I went on to do lots of Zandra's shows – much to my grandma's delight. She'd watch the videos of them on repeat of and was overjoyed when some snaps of me in ballgowns appeared in *Hello!* magazine. Nigel dubbed me 'the new Audrey Hepburn', and got me enough work to keep me going while I looked for a job writing for a newspaper. I was delighted that my height (5 foot 11), which had made me the odd one out among the girls at school, and not feminine and petite enough for boys, had suddenly become an asset for which I was paid. It was an exciting new experience to be backstage at shows, necking coffee and champagne at 7 a.m., or catching the Tube eating fried chicken in a takeaway box, still while sporting an outrageous hairstyle and full show make-up, accompanied by girls just as lanky as I was. It's an undeniably great feeling when whatever it is that makes you weird suddenly transforms into an advantage (a feeling I was to experience later in football).

After almost a year, I ditched the shows and photo shoots for a newspaper job. Following a two-week trial on the *Grimsby Evening Telegraph*, the *Essex Chronicle* called and I relocated to Chelmsford. The job was in the sales department, rather than editorial, and it came with a blue and white Ford van, lots of A-boards and the chance to create great relationships with various newsagents from Billericay to Southend. Though I'd wanted to be a journalist, I consoled myself with the thought that writing for newspapers might be beyond my capabilities anyway. However, despite enjoying the more creative aspect of the role – writing my 'Newsagent of the Week' piece for the paper's various sister publications and inventing ways to shift more copies – I found sales less motivating after a time, though I was good at the relationship side: one newsagent took me to a London casino, another attended Buddhist meetings with me, and yet another introduced me to the (surprisingly massive) folk music scene in Essex pubs.

Soon after the job started, a friend of mine took his own life back in London. Devastated, in a new town and unsure what to do with my shock and grief, I rang the Samaritans. I ended up going to see them for a cuppa, and after some weeks of very good training became a volunteer on the phones. More motivated by my evenings than the day job, I decided to change my career plan and train as a counsellor instead.[6] So after just one year in Essex, I returned to London. I found a counselling course that chimed with my Buddhism-influenced beliefs about people and change, and signed up with yet another model agency to pay my rent and the course fees. I now felt I'd found a purpose. Helping people navigate their feelings and understand themselves better seemed, at that point, more valuable than selling newspapers.

Over the next few years, I lived a kind of double life. My weekdays were spent rushing around London going to castings and modelling jobs, while at the weekend I trained to be a counsellor at the Metanoia Institute in Ealing. I was also holding down a volunteer job at a therapy centre on Thursdays. Sometimes there wasn't time to remove glitter from skin or varnish from nails before seeing a client, and some would comment on my weekly haircuts and drastic colour changes (I had a regular Sunday job for Wella, who paid me well for the use of my head to demonstrate haircuts to hairdressing students, and I emerged with a shorter hairstyle every week).

I was the youngest person in my cohort at Metanoia training for a diploma in person-centred counselling, and sometimes felt a bit out of my depth when my peers talked about a plethora of life events I hadn't yet encountered. I studied and experienced what it was to have congruent, empathic relationships characterised

---

6   I'd had counselling while at university when a doctor diagnosed me with an 'anxiety complex'. It had been a transformative experience – constant tension headaches had 'magically' disappeared after I was facilitated to express previously unexpressed anger.

by unconditional positive regard. The training was both healing and unsettling, requiring us to be vulnerable with each other in order to establish that all-important human quality – trust. I also attended my own one-to-one counselling sessions, and group therapy too, for a number of years.

Therapy circles, which emphasised our value as individual human beings, were worlds apart from my day job, where I was often a 'piece of meat' or a 'clothes hanger' with no voice or personal agency. As a model, I did as I was told, had no say in the final shot or show, suppressed feelings and needs (sometimes a toilet break wasn't possible if I was in an outfit and everyone else on set was ready) simply to be rebooked. My smiles were constantly on tap. In striking juxtaposition, as a trainee counsellor, my feelings and needs were reflected back to me and acted upon wherever possible. I had agency, I expressed myself as fully as I could, and I was taught to look after and care for myself. I only smiled when I felt the urge, and not to order. I was aware of, and even got a kick out of, the stark contrast. Writing about it now, having a foot in two contrasting worlds also feels like a portent for the work I would do in football in the future.

While modelling, I was acutely aware that I dissociated myself from the image I was asked to project for clients. I could be 'sexy', or 'strong', or 'soft', but it wasn't really me, of course – just a deliberately conjured image which met a client's specific request. And the clients were as diverse as wonderful designers or companies making everything from books to drinks, to make-up, to hairdryers. I had regular bread-and-butter jobs with various hair companies, worked as a house model for British designer Ally Capellino and appeared in seasonal student shows with colleges, as well as walking for designers like Hussein Chalayan, Pam Hogg and John Galliano. Later in life, the learned ability to pose unselfconsciously and with intent came in useful while coaching embarrassed female football players to perform off the pitch. It's awkward when a camera is thrust in front of you and empowering to know how to take a mental step back and handle it. Modelling also gave me a bit of a head start in performing, when football would suddenly require me to get up on stages and speak publicly.

On finishing my counselling training, I landed a job as an internal counsellor for PolyGram Records. I was 24. 'Jammy' was the word used by peers from my training cohort. Human resources told me I got the job because I was 'young and the other interviewees had worn Laura Ashley dresses and Tampax earrings' ('Staff at record companies just won't relate to those people!' they said, so lucky me!). Pushing imposter syndrome aside, my colleague Melissa Darmody and I did everything we could to make PolyGram's counselling service work, even though initially we had no designated space in which to offer actual therapy! We hit the ground running, seeing clients in a bathroom, outside on a bench in Hammersmith and in music execs' private offices. We counselled in London and Essex, recruiting and building a team of affiliate counsellors who could do the same in other locations where the company had factories or offices. We could offer only eight sessions to each employee in a year, so we built up a referral service, familiarising ourselves with all kinds of diverse therapies for clients going forward, and specifically training in solution-focused brief therapy. PolyGram were forward-thinking, the service was in demand and we were breaking new ground.

When Melissa relocated to Dublin to work in rape crisis, I inherited sole responsibility for the 24/7 telephone line based at my flat for potential clients from any of PolyGram's offices or companies. I soon got used to justifying my budget to PolyGram UK's financial director each month. 'Prove to me that people here are happier as a result of your service!' he'd say from behind his large desk, freaking me out with his challenging directness and the power dynamic created by his greater experience in the industry. And after a couple of months of scratching my head about how on earth to prove happiness, I'd give him collated attendee numbers and anonymous feedback forms, to back up the need for, and success of, the thriving service. In the music industry, many presenting problems were connected to alcohol, drugs and/or the difficulty of maintaining long-distance relationships. But there were also plenty of people who just needed somewhere safe to let off steam and share their burdens. It was intense but ultimately rewarding work. And PolyGram were generous employers who paid me on exactly the same level as any other manager. I was glad to be able to develop myself fully there in my chosen profession, learning an awful lot about therapy within organisations and the importance of boundaries, outside networks and support.

I didn't go back to PolyGram after maternity leave – it was

too full-on with a young baby to look after as well. However, I expanded a private practice, eventually stopping therapy work altogether due to illness, and then the birth of my second child.

When we moved to Lewes in 2007, I was able, finally, to develop my writing by blogging about fashion, and briefly being a producer/presenter for a local TV channel (again useful experiences for my future work in the beautiful game). I had articles published by HuffPost and various online magazines, and a cover feature for the *Observer* magazine. But by then life had taken another turn, and I had become – of all things – a fan of Lewes FC.

Chapter 4
Unwelcome Women

_If women do not attain roughly equal fame and
fortune in sports, it leads both men and women
to think of women as naturally inferior._

Jane English, academic

I asked a lot of questions of Charlie and Ed in the weeks that
followed their groundbreaking decision and my epiphany. I read
a book, recommended by Ed, called _Girls With Balls_ by Tim Tate
(since changed – presumably to avoid confusion or defamation –
to _Women's Football: The Secret History_). The _Daily Mail_ have
called the book 'Witty, well-written and deeply sympathetic – a
fitting monument for . . . all the intrepid women who turned out
to play the beautiful game in the teeth of male scorn.' If you are
confused by teeth, so am I. Maybe the males were so vocal with
their scorn that their teeth became bigger than their faces? Given
some of the comments I've since seen from male fans of men's
football on social media, it really wouldn't surprise me. I was

already getting the impression that many men were defensive about football, wanting to lay claim to it as their own, as a woman-free zone.

I learned that during the First World War, when the men went off to fight, the women were put to work in munitions factories, making weapons and parachutes to support the war effort. During their breaks, some of them started to kick a ball around in the factory yards. Factories began to play against each other after work, night shifts challenged day shifts to matches, and a lot of competitive fun was had. Teams started to become organised, and although the press treated the women's games as a novelty for the male gaze ('all the players "looked tasty". Good looks predominated and generally the thought of most of the men present was "How happy could I be with either were t'other dear charmer away"', according to the *Essex Newsman*), they grew to fill a hole in the market vacated by the men who'd gone to war. Crowds were large, and although the women's teams were ridiculed at first, for their clothes and their invasion of traditionally male space, they soon began to be taken more seriously. Certainly the takings at the gate were appreciated, as almost all the money was donated to charities for ex-servicemen and poor families.

Stars emerged, Lily Parr of the Dick, Kerr Ladies foremost among them. Two things about Lily stick in my mind: it was said that she once asked to be paid in Woodbines for her efforts, and she could break a goalie's limb with one strike of the ball. Something about reported facts like these makes me, with my slightly weedy, sometimes fragile body, feel a bit stronger. A player of character and strength, Lily is currently the only woman to have a statue in her honour in the National Football Museum in Manchester (and a floodlight I named after her at the Dripping Pan, of course, where she will light up a pitch in perpetuity).

When the men returned from the war, they couldn't muster the same crowds as the now very popular women, even by their second full season back. This was when the FA held their now infamous meeting banning women from playing the game on FA pitches or with FA-affiliated coaches, effectively destroying women's football in one fell swoop, and squashing all the hopes and passions of those who loved to play it. That ban lasted 50 years, and it would be another 22 years before the FA deigned to establish an official women's committee. This meant that 'over the entire period in which the iconography of men's football was being created and imprinted on our country's culture, women's football to all intents and purposes did not exist', as Ed articulated it to me. He also pointed out that 'When Geoff Hurst scored his hat-trick in 1966 to win us the World Cup, there was no competing female narrative to capture the collective imagination – to fire the dreams of young girls in England – because women hadn't been allowed to play for the last 45 years! And we talk about 50 years of hurt for the *men's* England team!'

It's amazing, isn't it, how unearthing historical facts can make you feel about the present. I had a strong suspicion that these facts had been *deliberately* submerged, because gender inequality was a convenient situation for the government to reinstate after the First

World War,[7] and no doubt benefited our patriarchal economy. Babies were needed, childcare was needed, and so upstart women were 'put back in their place' and all was good in the historic hood, as it were.

I discovered that men's football – the sport that had had the monopoly on sponsorships, minds and, crucially, lucrative broadcasting rights for that significant time – currently had something like 3.6 billion fans around the world. I knew that most of these fans were men. I understood England to be a major competitor on the global footballing stage. And, in 2017, I also knew that statistics for violence against women and girls were increasing, and that, globally, women were being treated as lesser citizens, even in so-called progressive nations. I knew there was a gender pay gap in 2017–18 of 17 per cent (which has risen to 21.8 per cent in 2023). The hashtag #MeToo, started by Tarana Burke in 2006 to help black women who had been sexually abused band together and stand up for themselves, gained more traction in 2017 when actress Alyssa Milano urged victims of sexual harassment to share their stories on social media. It made shocking reading, alongside stories closer to home, where many of the teenage girls (and boys) I knew were suffering around the issue of consent and a perceived lack of agency to change anything. Kids made 'rapey' jokes in schools. Anxiety was common and growing among teens. Girls' participation in sports was low for a myriad reasons. I could go on. To me, the sexist football facts and

---

7 · The 1919 Restoration Act.

the misogynistic cultural issues were not at all unrelated. Change one, we could change the others.

For too long in my own life, I had spoken with other women about glass ceilings, unfair distribution of domestic chores, the price and quality of childcare and the fear of walking home alone at night. And as Rachel Hewitt says in her excellent book *In Her Nature*, 'Sport is never "just sport". The ability to participate and be powerful in sport is directly linked to the ability to participate and be powerful in public life.' Here was a chance, through a sport that men loved with a passion, to talk to *them* about gender inequality. Because men were the gender who appeared to be in charge in real terms, who needed to understand and care in order to bring about real transformation.

Against this background, Equality FC was publicly introduced, with a now iconic video in which another club owner, comedian Dave Lamb, asks viewers: 'How do you tell your daughter she's worth less than your son?' while sweaty, focused girls play football behind him on the pitch at the Dripping Pan. He goes on to explain that Lewes FC have decided to pay and resource their women's team the same as their men's, 'So *you* don't have to tell *your* daughter that stuff.' The short film was designed to engage male fans on the subject of gender equality through their relationships with their daughters.

Equality FC made national and international headlines. Most people, ultimately fair-minded, found the idea refreshing and revolutionary. But there were critics. And – it has to be said – they were all men. They argued that the club shouldn't pay the women the same as the men because they didn't get the same 'gate'. 'Gate' is football parlance for takings at the turnstiles. Now this was true, but due to what I have come to coin 'male football privilege', most people didn't know when or where women's games were being played, and were anyway – thanks to that ban they were affected by but largely unaware of – unused to the idea of going to watch women's games. It simply wasn't a thing. So the gate figure was an unfair comparison and one that the club needed to address. However, as Charlie lamented to me, there were no women on the board willing to systematically go and tell other women about what the club was trying to do and ask them to come to women's games in solidarity. Oh, and didn't I know a lot of women's groups? Fired up by my inaugural experience of watching women's football, and angry about the history, Reader, I took the bait.

At this point there were in fact a couple of very involved women on the board. Women who were football fans and had themselves played the game for periods in their lives. They were huge supporters of the women's team but were too busy – or not in a position – to start drawing up lists and going to talk to people. They'd also served on the board for some time and were close to either stepping down or resigning. It's regrettable, but in the time I've been associated with the club, the board has had a knack for burning people out, and has (like most football clubs) a particularly low uptake and retention rate for female members.

One of these women was Jacquie Agnew, who had captained the team when they were still (nearby) Ringmer Ladies, and who had, with the help of local businessman Ron Moore, and Lewes FC chair at that point, Terry Parris, brought them over to Lewes for the 2002–3 season, and proceeded to win trophies and coach them up the leagues to the point where they were the jubilant warriors they were in 2017.

Personally, I still felt cross that I'd been deliberately excluded (without knowing it) from a national pastime on the basis of, well, not having a penis. I was also livid that I'd been led to assume that, *somehow*, women, including myself, were inherently inferior at this sport that had accrued so much power and influence among men. At the same time, I was so inspired by this move for social justice from my local football club and so concerned for my children and the narcissistic, gendered online culture they and their generation lived in that I was ready to pick up a loudspeaker and walk the streets if I had to – Lewes FC's risk *had* to pay off because it was about so much more than football. Our society – men, women, girls, boys – needed to perceive women as powerful agents of their own lives rather than objects or decorations, and just as importantly, to let boys off their strong, stoic, inexpressive hook. Maybe there would be more female bosses and fewer male suicides as a result, I figured. As a society, didn't we need to move beyond these unhelpful stereotypes? And football, with such a committed male following, was an excellent place to begin a culture shift.

Thus, I gamely started with my surprised local friends, badgering them, gently at first and then relentlessly, about how Lewes FC would change the world for women and how they had to lend their support by coming to a match with me. And, bless them, they started to come. There was fun to be had cheering and chatting in the terraces. Many's the time I'd chuckle to myself hearing a couple of men behind us analysing the match while we were debating anything from where to get the best vitamin C supplements to the non-duality of religion, to, you know, mild vaginal prolapse. Those terraces at the Pan have heard it all, believe me. And though a few friends dropped off (women's matches are on Sunday afternoons – untouchable family time for some), many continued on the journey to consistent fandom. It's important to note that these were women who hadn't been interested in football before, but gave it a try because they believed in the cause of gender equality. They gradually changed their own behaviours and perspectives by coming back . . . again and again.

Encouraged by my friends' reactions, I began to think about reaching out to women's groups. It wouldn't be hard to attract interest, surely, because people were curious. After all, Lewes FC were making headlines. 'Lewes FC become first professional club to pay women and men equally,' reported the *Guardian*, adding, 'East Sussex club launches groundbreaking initiative' and 'There should be a level playing field for women in football.' While on the BBC they talked about 'the football club with no gender pay gap'. Local and national TV had been down to the Pan for the 'Equality FC' announcement, reporting back with defiant and inspirational quotes from directors and the women's manager, Jacquie Agnew: 'You can't say it's impossible to introduce equality to football any more, because we've done it.'

People seemed generally impressed that women footballers at Lewes would be paid the same as men, have the same marketing resources behind them, benefit from the same standard of coaching and continue to play on the same pitch in their home town. And at the same time, the men wouldn't lose out because directors had agreed to take the hit of raising the women's budget to meet the men's, rather than lowering the men's. This practical solution to the playing budgets is another important point to note, because one of the issues that came up repeatedly from some existing men's fans was whether the introduction of equality would mean that those who had benefited from *in*equality would now be short-changed. We could reassure them that they wouldn't be, and introduced the slogan (which now stands proudly under the TV gantry at the Dripping Pan, thanks to a grant from the local town council), 'Equality is a rising tide that lifts all boats.'

I think my first public talk was fairly casually delivered, at our local Lewes Women in Business group. I emphasised that just like women in business, women in football were marginalised and often had to put in extra effort, make extra sacrifices, to do the thing they wanted to do. And how normal this was. The women related. I shared some facts about how much female footballers (didn't) earn compared to men, some of the vast (yet run-of-the-mill) gender-based disparities in the game, and the little-known history of women's football in this country. I saw jaws dropping around the room. I explained that the more I found out, the more it seemed to me that sexism really was the wallpaper of football – there for everyone to see, but unquestioned until now (and by relatively small Lewes FC). It was true, the club's recent groundbreaking announcement had unearthed little-known facts and started conversations about women's status in football. I pointed out that we were hearing a lot about gender inequality generally – pay gaps, impractically gendered school uniforms, violence against women and girls – and were often concerned for our daughters at school and in the workplace, but that usually we were powerless to do anything about any of it. Now I offered them a chance to take action. 'By coming to a women's game, or becoming an owner of Lewes FC, you are contributing to a movement that will see women fairly treated and smash stereotypes on a significant stage. What Lewes FC Women achieve on the pitch can now affect us all off the pitch and in any business where men are involved – yes, that's most businesses. This will change the way we all think about women and even, if my experience is anything to go by, about our own selves.'

It was like offering crisp white wine spritzers to parched throats on a hot summer's evening. The women came to matches and/or bought a single share to become owners of the football club. Some of those who turned up on the terraces didn't even like sport generally, never mind football. But it seemed that all these women had experienced sexism, and they all wanted to support their footballing sisters, who were symbolic of the change they yearned for.

With more female club owners signing up, I made lists of other organisations, in Lewes, Brighton and London. Alongside our new part-time female marketing manager, Rosy Matheson, I set up stalls at a couple of women's conferences, with Lewes FC merchandise and information about Equality FC. Our mouths and faces ached by the end of the day, but it felt like an excellent use of time and energy when we saw how inspired other women were by, of all things, a football club! They'd come up to us, sheepishly eyeing our football scarves and baseball caps, and we'd win them over with friendliness and facts. We sold more ownerships – some women buying them for themselves, and some as presents – and we realised, from the delighted feedback of activist women, that this was probably one of the most progressive gifts anyone could give: a share in a football club that was enacting gender equality – the best £30[8] you could ever spend! It was clear from the reaction that feminist football club ownership had the potential to become a movement, if only we could keep reaching more and more of the fair-minded, or the plain pissed-off!

'Tell us about events in *your* area over the weekend!' requested a local radio presenter as I listened in my car back in November 2017. Not one to look the gift horse of a potential new market in the mouth, I pulled over, called in to BBC Radio Sussex's afternoon show and told listeners about the forthcoming Lewes FC Women's match happening the following Sunday at the Pan. On air, I got into an extended conversation with the friendly host, Allison Ferns, about the history of women's football. She was super interested, asking all the right questions, exclaiming in disbelief in all the right places. When she grasped that the

---

8   Now £50.

inequality we were experiencing in football by not knowing about women's matches and only hearing about men's had been entirely and intentionally constructed by a sexist decision made by a group of men back in 1921, she was genuinely surprised. Afterwards, her producer emailed me to say that Allison had invited me to come on every week to report on the women's match, and more, she would like to officially adopt Lewes FC Women as her team for the afternoon show. This was unexpected and wonderful news. But it also filled me with dread. Had BBC Radio Sussex made the mistake of thinking I was a seasoned football fan who knew how the game worked? I emailed back explaining that 'I'm not sure I can really be a football pundit as I know very little about the rules of football!' The producer promptly replied, 'Well, neither do our listeners! Allison thinks it'll be great!'

A little concerned that the phrase 'the blind leading the blind' kept popping into my head, I found myself agreeing to the idea. 'Winging it is just another name for pioneering!' encouraged Charlie, laughing. And so I added 'football pundit' to my increasingly weird CV, much to the delight of my husband, male friends and cousins and anyone I knew who liked football and was aware of the true extent of my knowledge of the game. They all thought it was very funny, but it wasn't them with butterflies battering their insides before going on air every Monday, was it?

Charlie talked about the 'three tectonic plates' – *attention, sponsorship* and *crowds* – that needed to move in order for the women's game to reach its potential, and I could see that the media was a big part of *attention,* and that a local radio show could be a good way to attract both crowds and sponsorship. All three areas needed to move together in order to rejig the system and reposition women's football as the huge growth product it was poised to be.

Not to risk embarrassment on live radio, I used my car journeys to Lewes FC women's away games with Ed and Charlie to gen up on the game of football itself and get background information. I'd ask about opposing teams and clubs, getting stats on their (lack of) fans and stadia. On the way back, I'd listen avidly to their dissection of the game, and pick up various phrases about 'bad refereeing decisions', players being 'evenly matched' and how 'getting one in early doors would have made all the difference'. Then the following day I'd gamely chat to Allison. I *was* winging it, but as gate figures edged steadily upwards, the ruse seemed to be working.

Sometimes Allison and I would chat about the match, sometimes about a story from the club (a quote from a fellow volunteer, or a player talking from the inside about football), a new campaigning activation, or a group I'd spoken to (by now I was regularly addressing various Women's Institute (WI) groups, Women's Equality Party branches and other local women's organisations). I'd bang on about visits to Brighton Women's Centre, UN Women UK, TV appearances, or the obstacles standing in plucky Lewes' path. Admittedly my match reports included tales of the excellent quality of the brioche buns we used for burgers, the characterful canine visitors to the Pan, and new attractions introduced to cater to our emerging new market at women's games, with a strategy that would generate that all-important 'customer stickiness', ensuring that these matchday virgins would return. Allison and her audience were entertained with tales of the newly introduced Prosecco on tap,[9] the free chocolates for mums on Mother's Day, the matchday themes, the pre-match choirs (and their friends), the cleverly angled posters, and all the off-pitch details that Charlie, Ed, the part-time staff and I were constantly thinking about and adding to the mix, as we tried different ideas to appeal to the sector I was now dubbing 'unwelcome women'. I'd consult Charlie about the matches whenever possible so that I could also speak at least fairly knowledgeably about our opponents and the style of play. To be fair, we were changing the culture, Allison was helping, and it was happening conversation by conversation. Listeners were interested in this new development at Lewes FC and consequently in women's football.

Once or twice when Allison was away, I'd speak to her male stand-ins.

'So, you've got the Millwall Lionesses[10] coming on Sunday, Karen? You must be a bit worried.'

'Well, yes, they are a couple of places above us in the table, but the Rooks manager tells me he's making some changes to our formation and that should deal with it.'

---

9   This was a fun way to tell women they were welcome, but became unexpectedly popular among male fans. One of the first manifestations of our slogan, 'Equality is a rising tide that lifts all boats'!

10 The Millwall Lionesses left Millwall in 2019 to become the independent London City Lionesses. They are now thriving under Michele Kang's investment and ownership.

The presenter laughed. 'No, I meant you must be a bit worried *given the fans' reputation!*'

'Oh, right,' I replied. 'Well the truth is, they don't seem to have many fans when we've played them at home.'

'Oh, so it's different on the women's side?'

It was clear we were talking at cross-purposes.

I came off air – ridiculously proud of myself for using the word 'formation' – to Charlie chuckling away about the miscommunication and filling me in on what the presenter had actually been referring to: that Millwall (men's) fans were synonymous with the worst kind of football aggression.

It was a source of amusement to many around me that my knowledge of football was being built entirely from the women's game, and I was, at this early stage in the journey anyway, effectively ignoring men's football. Karmic really – I was inadvertently doing to the men's game what it had done to me. Men's football just wasn't in my head. By the same token, the male presenter was thinking *only* in terms of the men's game, as the women's game wasn't in *his* head. But though both men and women play football, the actual games are, for many reasons, quite different subjects, not to mention experiences.

Chapter 5
Team Talk

So many of us have gotten ourselves to the table,
but we're still too grateful to be there to really shake it up.

Michelle Obama

By now I'd taken to going down to the Dripping Pan or hanging out at the all-weather 3G pitch to chat to the women players at training. I had also interviewed a couple of them for various local publications. An understanding of what motivated female players, their stories in life and in football, their needs and hopes, was essential to my ability to do the kind of authentic promotion that I wanted to do. Sensitive to the fact that this was a new world about which I knew little, I was humble and curious, well aware there was a lot to learn. Around this time, we all (as in Ed, Charlie, Rosy and myself) felt I needed a title to validate the type and amount of work I was doing and lend me authority, so I was officially 'volunteer press officer'.

With humility in mind, I want to explain what a 3G pitch is when it's at home. Its name is short for third generation, and you can play there any time because the ground isn't grass, but rather a surface of synthetic turf, sand and rubber. I've noticed that football people might ask you if a pitch is 3G or 4G. Which means either that they don't understand how impressive it is that you actually know what a 3G is, *or* that they're trying to impress you with their own expertise and swag. Either way, don't respond. The club crowdfunded – alongside grants from Sport England and the Football Foundation – to build the Lewes 3G, and as we could remind so many about so much within football, it's not there to boost anyone's ego but as a community resource.

One day I was sitting with a few players pitchside when one of the club's regular volunteers approached. I'd already built up respect for him because he did loads of work around the place as well as holding down a full-time job. He was there at the club most mornings early, and then after work again, and back at weekends keeping things in great shape for every match. A legend. What's more, unlike some of the other male volunteers, he was always up for a chat, making me feel welcome. I asked him the same question I asked everyone those days, 'You coming to the match on Sunday?'

'What, the ladies' match?'

'Yes!' (I didn't correct the patronising-sounding 'ladies' at first, as we weren't quite at that stage of the journey, Lewes only just having changed from 'Lewes Ladies' to 'Lewes Women'. We were trying to drop 'the Rookettes' tag too – we were all Rooks here, not lesser than the male players, however cute it sounded.)

'Nah. I'd rather watch the county boys than the ladies,' came the smiling answer.

'Oh' was all I could say before he walked off.

I was gutted. Three or four female players had been in earshot of the conversation. Mostly they seemed to shrug it off. I guess because he was very likeable and worked long, valuable hours for the club: we couldn't have done without him. Or maybe because they'd heard comments like that a million times before and the exchange was completely unremarkable. Shannon Moloney, a fiery midfielder, had gone uncharacteristically quiet, and seeing her face, I had to ask how she'd felt when he said that. She looked at me. 'I'm fuming,' she replied, eyes flashing. 'I couldn't've said a word to him,' she continued, 'or I might have blown someone's head off.'

I remember this incident clearly because of the emotions attached to it, and because of what happened five years later. I remember witnessing Shannon's anger and noting that I'd put mine aside in favour of engagement. It felt like an awkward moment, the kind that was to replay in my head at 3 a.m. for many nights. I totally empathised with Shannon but knew that the subject of her wrath was exactly the kind of person we needed to stay in good communication with if he and others like him were to be open to changing the way they viewed women's football. And I was sure we wouldn't achieve anything but hurt by having a go or getting too obviously angry. Not with this volunteer anyway!

I recalled this moment fondly when the very same man came up to me five years down the line at Lewes Town Hall. We were enjoying an evening of speeches by myself and others for councillors and local community leaders about the club's purpose. We were drinking Prosecco together (not the first time!), and he nudged me on the arm to signal he wanted a chat. 'When you first came to the club, I thought you were coming in to try to change things. Kind of intimidating. But now I can see that what you're doing is really good for the club.' He looked genuinely moved. I was genuinely moved too, but could only guess that it had been my height that was intimidating, because back then I had felt very far from the strident woman he was depicting. We hugged, and in that moment, I felt the real impact of the work we were doing.

Since then, I've realised it probably wasn't my height that had made him uneasy around me. It was more likely the fact that I was a woman who didn't know football the way he did, and that I appeared to be in a position of power. As such, I was a threat. Once he had got to know me, and seen the effects of some of my work, he was much happier. Also, incidentally, at the time of writing, he now comes to a few women's games, occasionally letting off fireworks. I am not speaking figuratively – this is Lewes, after all, and he's a proud 'Bonfire Boy'.

The other tangible result of this incident in 2018 was that I identified Shannon as a person with passion in her heart and a story to tell, and invited her to the next talk I was doing – to a businesswomen's club in Brighton. I asked her to share obstacles she'd had to overcome in order to play football at this semi-pro level. Although she'd not done a public speech about her journey before, and was nervous, she was very up for it, and wrote down her experience immediately. She emailed me what she was planning to say. Her story was personal and shocking.

It was a dark, rainy night when 'Shaz', with her partner and her partner's mum along for support, met me near the seafront. We went to a newly decorated three-storey town house, surrounded by buzzy restaurants and boutiques in the shopping area of Brighton. It still smelled of paint inside, as well as perfume and booze. We were given special gin cocktails by the event sponsor, and the four of us cheersed together, a little giggly, a little wary of the grand environment, and our objective, before too long, to 'own the room'.

'You OK?' I asked Shaz.

'Bit shaky,' she replied, clutching her glass.

She needn't have worried. As she spoke, Shannon Moloney had the smartly dressed audience of professional young women in their twenties and thirties sat in the rather imposing room crying into their complimentary cocktails.

They listened to how this little girl had loved football and played it simply to be her authentic self. They were appalled at the treatment that Shannon – describing herself as 'a Cockney-ish girl who looks Indian, with the native wit of my Irish genes, and a wicked right foot' – said she had received from football (at top level), and emotional hearing about the difficulties she'd overcome to play the game she loved and to be a role model to other girls who wanted to play football. Blocked at every turn, unsupported by her club for medical care when compared to a male colleague, she soon saw there was a higher purpose to her passion and her anger. She explained that she had been a policewoman (but left because of sexism in the force), and had taught A level law – both while playing football to an elite standard and training at night! The lack of pay, kit and medical support she received was criminal. 'You would not send a builder to work without the correct tools, as they would not be able to complete their job, yet these huge football clubs whose revenue is in the millions allow their women's team to use the same training shirt four times a week. As fantastic as we women are,' she joked with the audience, getting into her swing, 'I have to tell you that we do actually sweat! We have had to "put up and shut up" at clubs for far too long.' It was the last straw when Shannon shared that she wasn't allowed to make a cup of tea in the same kitchen as players from the men's team at one club, and yet the women's team weren't given any kitchen space. What did our firecracker do? Made a cup of effing tea for herself anyway! We cheered!

Sharing her story, as well as personal details from her family life, moved everyone, including me. There was simply no way a male footballer playing at Shannon's level would have been treated like that – we all knew it. In my heart I resolved again to get a better deal for these amazing women whom clubs had routinely shafted. In *their* hearts, the audience resolved to support Lewes FC and our equality campaign. Shannon and I did more talks together after that – judging by the tweets and emails, 'Shaz and Kaz' went down quite well!

But what about the players who weren't so angry? The ones who shrugged it all off and put up with it?

The first thing to say about the female players at Lewes FC may sound a little strange, but at that point, in my early days at the club, they rarely seemed angry enough to me. Coming from outside the footballing environment as I did, I remained constantly agog at the sexist structures they were required to work within. Yes, sexism abounded all around us – in business, in fashion, in the music industry, in the film industry, in politics, in the media – but never had I seen or heard of such *blatant* sexism in terms of pay, resources and treatment. Football seemed to put so many otherwise aware people to sleep when it came to basic human rights!

Sometimes I'd accidentally 'radicalise' players with the statistics I was uncovering about the gender-based disparity in the FA Cup prize, or news stories about Ballon d'Or winner Ada Hegerberg being asked to 'twerk' by a male presenter, or Andy Murray repeatedly and quietly calling out sexist questions in post-match interviews, or the Irish national women's team being forced to change out of kit in airport toilets because the Irish FA wouldn't provide enough tracksuits, and after these chats, the players would leave more fired up than they had been half an hour before. They'd also remember incidents they'd buried in their minds, because previously what had been the point of complaining about a pretty much fixed status quo? It usually got you either nowhere, or benched (not selected to play in a match), or even kicked out of a team. Coming from a non-football background meant *I* saw these constant stories with new and horrified eyes, while experience had taught these women that such disrespectful treatment was normal. The truth was that by now in their careers, they expected all this – for female footballers, indignities and injustice were simply part of the scenery.

Imagine you're a toddler who likes kicking a ball, but your parents keep shoving dolls and ballet kits in front of you (Lewes captain Rhian Cleverly). Imagine you're a little girl who plays well, but the boys at school won't let you join in (Lewes forward Katie Rood). Imagine you love the game but have to join a boys' team and parents yell at their sons not to pass to a girl (Lewes defender Amy Taylor). Imagine your school gives all the boys the afternoon off to watch the men's world cup, but despite your pleas, and the fact that you already play in the England set-up and are the best footballer in the school, you and the other girls are forced to stay in lessons (Lewes midfielder Paula Howells). Imagine you finally find a female team to practise with but someone has to drive you there and back three long nights a week because it's so far away (Lewes goalie Faye Baker). Imagine you qualify for a club team but are given pitches to train on where you and your teammates have to pick up goose poo before you can play (Lewes under-18s captain Amy Critchfield).

Imagine you have to pay to play while the men at your club are given free cars and extra kit (Lewes winger Sammy Quayle). Imagine you have to put on a wash every night to have clean football socks, because you have a day job to get to in the morning and training tomorrow night and the club have only given the women one set of kit compared to the men's five (Lewes midfielder Shannon Moloney). Imagine that all the posters in your bedroom are of male football stars because there aren't any of women

(Lewes striker Jess King). Imagine you only get 15 minutes to eat in the club canteen if the men go over their 45 minutes (a whole team at a renowned club). Imagine having to play in the ill-fitting men's kit from a previous season (most female players at that time). Imagine your club get a great sponsor who makes football boots but you're not even allowed to *buy* them because they're just for the men (Jess King again). Imagine you seriously damage your knee at the same time as your male counterpart on the men's team, but recovery takes you two years and him six months because the club doesn't pay for you, so you have to fund your own treatment (Shannon Moloney again). And after all this discouragement, all the fight you've had to muster, all the work you've had to do and the sacrifices and effort you've made, you're so grateful to be allowed to play the sport you love, and get any sort of remuneration for it, that you don't question any of these things because it's just how it is and you just want to play! *Please!* Well, that's how it was for most female players back in 2017, and still is for many now, though things are changing, at least at the better-funded top of the game.

You see, to compete at this level, these women had been in football since they were little girls, and it had *never* been hassle-free. They'd been marginalised since they were very young by schools, friends, playgrounds, parks, coaches, parents, all of whom seemed not to want girls to play. And then by previous clubs, who'd casually 'removed funding' for their women's teams, or not included them in sponsorship deals, or made them pay to play, or given them inferior pitches to play on, or not looked after them medically, or given them men's kit to play in, or not paid for their travel, and so on and so on . . . The chronic ubiquity of unequal treatment had become normalised and an expected part of their lives.

As these players were my constant inspiration on the pitch, I needed to advocate. I wanted to show up this mistreatment for what it was, knowing that like-minded people would protest by supporting Lewes FC. Together we'd shine a light on the inequalities, elevate these women and help to fix the problem. It's funny, because previously just the thought of football would have made me bored, but now I had to laugh at myself! I was constantly thinking about the game and its implications – what had happened?!

I remember full-back Amy Taylor talking shyly with me at Sister Society in Brighton. Word was spreading and I'd accepted an invitation from this feminist group of young creatives for their monthly speaking slot. The audience were fashion-conscious, sustainability-minded young twenty-somethings with colourful clothes and hair and big smiles – about the furthest away you could get from your average football crowd back in 2018. My opening question was 'Does anyone here watch football?', and the answer was a resounding 'No!' A hard audience you might think for a talk about football and an invitation to a football match. Not at all. Once my chat about Equality FC enlightened them as to their general unwelcomeness at football clubs, and once I'd brought home to them that this was activism for the cause of gender equality, they were *raring* to get to the Pan. And once tracksuited Lewes defender Amy had told them that she wasn't used to talking in front of people but had overcome her nerves because she wanted to tell them how it felt to play football as a girl, and they had witnessed the truth of her quiet passion, well, that room could *not wait* for the next match! The young women were really impressed with the fact that Amy was an actual footballer, but also someone they could relate to. The compassion in the room was palpable. At the Q&A everyone wanted to ask a question, but at first, having been so enthralled by our stories, they weren't quite sure what to ask. And then they went for it . . .

'What do you do at the interval?' asked one voice.

'At *half-time* we're in the changing room listening to the manager and kind of encouraging each other,' said Amy.

'Do you wear the same for rehearsals as for the performance?' asked another.

'We get a training kit,' clarified Amy, chuckling a little.

'Do you have a special diet?'

'We've a nutritionist who tells us when to carb up and when to eat more protein.'

'How do you feel when you're playing football?'

'Really free. It's the only time when I don't have to worry about anything at all, except where the ball is.'

'Aah!' came the collective sigh of understanding round the room.

Chapter 6
Curious Women

Women ask more questions.

John Donoghue,
Lewes FC Women coach

I wasn't always lucky enough to bring a player along with me to talks. They were so busy working day jobs as well as playing football at weekends and training two or three nights a week, and I was acutely aware that I needed to be mindful of their energy levels, while balancing that with their development as professional people. And some players simply weren't keen on public speaking.

Speaking of training, coach John Donoghue also allowed me to go to the (then) twice-weekly evening training sessions and chat with injured players. These players weren't training but were still obliged to attend and support teammates. John and the coaching team (consisting back then of about three people) were kindly very accommodating when I asked a lot of questions, understanding that this was unfamiliar territory for me.

The players would start with a ten-minute warm up, then use resistance bands for another ten minutes to condition and activate the muscles; as the strength and conditioning coach told me, 'Most of the time when we're just walking, we're not really using our glutes, but when we're running we need to use them so we've got to work them in training.'

Right-o. Then came the 'unopposed technical passing practice', which is exactly what it says, so John looked at me quizzically when I asked him to break it down for me. He simply repeated the words slowly, then, taking pity, added, 'Well, it's *opposed* technical passing practice next, and they'll be using what they've learned. Does that help?'

It did. But things got more challenging – both on the pitch and off it – with me trying to get my non-sporty head around the growing puzzle. There was a collective physical and mental training session next, and then 'they get a lot of homework to do in the gym'. 'But,' John emphasised, 'if any team member has recently been to physio, there'll be an individual training session carefully worked out.'

I asked what 'mental training' was. John looked at me as if *I* was in fact mental. He explained that because the physical training mirrored an actual game as it progressed in terms of intensity, always increasing physical pressure on the girls, it was in itself mental training in endurance and determination.

I asked him the big question, the one I frequently asked myself: 'How has being paid equally impacted on the girls' game?'

'Well, if you asked them,' he replied, 'I think they'd say, "Getting paid better is good because it allows me to play football, but the conditions are just as important." They'd rather be at a supportive club, with great coaching, and not get paid. They want good training facilities. And then there's the fact that it doesn't actually *cost* them to play a game now. You see, a few years back, they were having to fork out about £25 a week just for the privilege of playing and training. And still drive miles and miles to get to games, and pay for their own transport as any transport provided was never enough for all of them. Things like that make a difference. They still have to pay for their own gym membership to do the training we give them. But Lewes is a great club to play for. Facilities like this' – he pointed to the all-weather 3G pitch – 'enhance what you can do. Here they play on the same pitch as the men, transport is provided, good changing facilities, a quality training pitch . . . It simply isn't like that for ladies' teams at other clubs.'

John went on to tell me that his team were 'very intelligent', comprising 'trainee dentists, PAs and university students'. He proudly added, 'And one is studying to be a prescribing pharmacist. That's almost a doctor.' I liked John a lot.

I asked what it was like as a man coaching women.

'I've coached both male and female teams, and in my experience the women ask more questions. They want to know *why*. Whereas the male players are more likely to just get on with it when they *should* ask why. Players learn more that way.'

Why did he think the women asked more questions?

'I reckon it's because they're generally educated to a higher level than the men I've coached. The men have played football and not concentrated on much else from the word go. But the women. They could never ever rely on "just football". That would be unrealistic. So they develop their minds in other areas, and have more enquiring attitudes as a result. They're more curious as to *why* I'm saying what I'm saying.'

The strength and conditioning coach, watching the players like a hawk as she spoke, enlightened me as to her role. 'My job is to prevent them getting injuries, and to make them stronger.' This sounded great to me, and I followed her gaze as she studied how the players were jumping and landing, carefully focusing on how their knees behaved. 'From this I can tell who needs to strengthen their glutes, and I'll set them work accordingly.'

I asked Faye Baker, the currently injured goalie – who would later help me in talks and engagement activities – about her footballing path. She was passionate about the game, willing to drop anything for football. 'Wherever I play I will move to a new house and a new town and get a new job for football. And if I can make one little girl fall in love with the game, then it's all been worth it. All the hours, all the sacrifices.'

Faye told me that she'd gone to an all-girls school that luckily supported her when she was chosen to play in the West Ham set-up – 'as long as I took my schoolwork with me'. 'I started when I was six, the only girl in an all-boys team, and at nine I was scouted for West Ham. Because I was at such a top club, I didn't have the social stigma problem that other girls at schools can get for playing football. I quit for four months when I was sixteen because a male manager knocked my confidence. But then, 'cos

I'd played for the county and at such a high level, I was scouted from all sides and went back.'

Faye struck me as hugely dedicated, and I was soon to learn that most female players at this level are – they've had to be to have come this far. What did she think about Equality FC?

'Well, women don't bring in the same revenue, but then we don't get the same publicity. People don't know when and where the games are. The men's game is more physical, but the women's is more *technical*, and also' – she chuckled, and her eyes lit up, about to say something characteristically cheeky – 'when they fall, the women just pull their socks up and get on with it!'

I asked about her current injury. It sounded awful. I winced when she told me she'd torn her quad in a recent game and then continued playing. She laughed. 'Yeah, but I literally play through anything. *And* I'll do anything for the game. If my coach told me to get up at four a.m. and run four miles, I would. To be a better footballer, I just would.'

Chapter 7
Being a Football Fan

You can't be what you can't see.

Marion Wright Edelman,

children's rights activist

Looking back, I believe a freezing-cold away fixture in Huddersfield was another personal turning point. For a variety of reasons. I'd been learning a lot about women's football, and was beginning to understand the jargon. I got a frisson of joy while watching live matches when I occasionally caught myself thinking in terms of hat-tricks, formations, creating space, tackling, volleying, possession, cautions and cards. Going to away matches, I was learning from both the strong contrast between the matchday experience at other clubs and that at Lewes FC, and from the inclusive camaraderie in a small group of fellow supporters. So when January 2018 saw us play Huddersfield away in the FA Cup, I was delighted to travel north on the train with Charlie, where we stayed at the same Premier Inn as the players, with a plan to meet Ed at the match the next day and all drive back to Lewes together in his car.

We saw the players off on their coach after a hearty breakfast of egg and bacon and all the trimmings – they needed to be at the ground earlier than us – then walked around town a little to kill some time and take in the beautiful historic market square and some throat-achingly cold winter air. A couple of hours later, I asked the hotel receptionist for a cab to take Charlie and me to the match. 'So that'll be to the John Smith Stadium?' she asked. This is the name of Huddersfield's men's football stadium – massive, complete with a beautiful pitch, conference facilities, events rooms and easy access from town.

'No,' I said. 'We're here to watch Huddersfield Ladies, and they're not allowed to play there. Strange, isn't it?' I was angling for a bit of sistership.

'Oh,' she replied. 'Where do *they* play then?'

I gave her the address, which was out of town and was in fact a disused university pitch. She looked surprised.

'My son plays under-11s rugby at the John Smith Stadium.' Now *I* was surprised. Surprised and appalled! So a young boy was allowed to play rugby on Huddersfield men's *football* pitch, but the women's football team weren't playing there? And consequently, we – women's football fans – weren't going there. I already felt lesser-than, both as a woman and as a women's football fan – and we hadn't even got there yet.

My feelings of anger increased as we drove out of town and up a dirt track, arriving at a slightly sloping field. It wasn't really a football stadium, but a poorly boundaried pitch with a small clubhouse nearby. Where, it turned out, they had already run out of food.

I stood there, frozen fingers pressing against a takeaway tea squeezing a memory of warmth, shouting, 'Come on, you Rooks!' at the top of my voice to some very determined women intent on defeating Huddersfield Ladies on this road to Wembley.

Going for yet another cuppa at half-time – for the cup temperature rather than its contents, you understand – I stood in a queue with some of the approximately 30 young tracksuited girls present, who played for the local juniors team. Mostly it looked like their dads had brought them along. One of them, Madison, brightly told me she wanted to play for England one day. In front of us in the queue was an FA scout (as was my wont, I'd already introduced myself to many of my fellow queuers), so I asked *her* what our young friend should do to achieve this ambition. 'Keep watching your elders,' came the immediate answer. 'You're in the right place!'

Hmm, I thought, this is the right place, is it? What does this place tell girls like Madison about their footballing ambitions? This is a place where they need to bring sandwiches because there are no hot pies. A place where there is little space to keep warm, no seating, little atmosphere. There seemed to be no easy way of getting here on public transport. What does this tell young Madison about what she has to look forward to, compared to her male counterpart watching Huddersfield Men in the John Smith stadium – or even playing there – with its impressive capacity, facilities, lights, food options, parading mascot, merchandising, you name it? Despite the cold, I felt the insult to women and girls deeply – and all the more so because it just seemed so *accepted*!

Post-match – we won 3–0 – I dissected the game with the other away supporters, feeling slightly smug that I knew what I was talking about. All seven (!) of us had bonded over our support for Lewes women's team, and we egged each other on in conversation until we'd completely analysed the match and were talked out: proud, happy and absolutely *right*, no question. Life was good. We knew what 'our girls' had done, and we knew why the other team couldn't hold a candle to them. 'Ah, Huddersfield were overconfident,' I said. 'Yes, resting on last season's laurels,' agreed Tim. 'Whereas we were well prepared. *Well* prepared. And *committed*!' added Kate, with her own commitment.

We all nodded, melting with pleasure in the shoddy bar area, anticipating and discussing the draw for the next match. It turned out there's lots to talk about when you hope and dream as one.

Ed, Charlie and I talked as well, the whole five and a half hours back down the motorway to Lewes. We'd lie on our pillows tonight that bit more satisfied than yesterday. It really was a great feeling, this 'being a football fan and winning' thing. Especially for Lewes fans, where our belief had the power to raise us all up, starting with women and girls.

As my hands thawed out under the hot taps of the ladies' loos in the motorway service station, I vowed once again that women's football should be better resourced. I noted that our team had also stopped off there to eat, as they had felt they hadn't had enough at

Huddersfield. Girls needed, of course, to see role models, but they must see them being paid, playing on beautiful pitches, flying first-class, driving nice cars, and with access to great coaches, medical staff, and good-sized portions of nutritionally balanced food! There really is nothing like an empty stomach, numb fingers and talking to a girl like young Madison to make a middle-aged woman, piecing together the personal and the political, want to activate and advocate. I reckon that as my fingers unfroze, so did my mind. I realised that I had something to offer women's football as an outsider in a still relatively small game. I couldn't accept the way things were, because I hadn't been groomed by the game to think of it all as normal. And at Lewes FC, the chance had been created to demonstrate a different 'normal'.

Chapter 8
Suffragette City

———

There is no art in turning a goddess into a witch, or a virgin
into a whore, but the opposite operation, to give dignity to what
has been scorned, to make the degraded desirable, that calls for
art or for character.

Goethe

Another freezing-cold Sunday in early 2018, and I'm standing
outside WHSmith in Lewes precinct, attempting to wear three
very long petticoats at once. They're warm, I'll say that for them,
but together they weigh a ton. Moving is awkward. Dancing will
be an accomplishment. On my head is a charity-shop straw hat
around which I've tied purple and green ribbons. The biting
wind has lent it a jaunty angle, but with its summer picnic vibe it
looks out of place in winter. I'm leaning against the shop wall in
a strategic position that affords me full visibility of the precinct.
Keeping very still, I wait, a large placard hidden behind my back.

The sign says 'Deeds Not Words, Equality FC' in big letters that still smell of my kids' marker pens.

Slowly walking towards me from various directions are around 30 miscellaneous local women, varying in age from 12 to 80. They sport similar costumes in the same colours – purple, green and white. Some look nervous, some determined; some, like me, I suspect, look slightly deranged. But underneath the high-necked blouses, prim coats and maxi underslips, we're all more than game. We're modern-day suffragettes – of course! – about to put into motion a flash mob dance routine, rehearsed over weeks in a church hall, to 'Sisters Are Doin' It for Themselves'. We're here to shimmy, we're here to shuffle, then we'll be off to march to the women's match.

We gather in small groups, talking away, pretending – as per the golden rule of the flash mob – that this is a normal Sunday morning, and that absolutely nothing out of the ordinary is about to happen.

W H Smith's staff have kindly agreed to let me run a wire for Charlie's massive stereo system from the street into their shop's electricity supply. We're waiting for our leader, Ginny Farman – friend, local mum and professional choreographer – to give us the nod and switch on the music, as we oh-so-casually linger and window-shop by Specsavers and New Look. Suddenly the first bars blare out and Annie Lennox's powerful voice starts to sing, 'Now there was a time, when they used to sa-ay . . .' We spring into action. Ginny has left room for creativity in the routine, and with each of Annie and Aretha's grunts, we're free to strike a pose of something a woman (read: human) might do. I act out digging with a spade for a few seconds, before switching to a bit of Man at C&A. (To anyone under 50, this means standing with one hand on your hip and the other perched over your forehead to shade your eyes as you gaze purposefully into the distance. Never let it be said that the years of modelling didn't come in useful.)

This street performance in our put-together suffragette costumes is one of the 'footballing' experiences I'll never forget. And there are videos to remind me. We did well with our unusual dance and poses – half of us footie fans, half decidedly not – and finished to loud cheers from unsuspecting passers-by that bracing February morning.

Afterwards, we gamely marched to the Pan, home-made banners and placards held aloft. We chanted as we walked, enjoying the attention, picking up people along the way and arriving at the turnstiles jubilant. We promptly made the front page of the following week's *Sussex Express*.

By now, dubbed alternately 'Equality FC campaign manager' and 'press officer', I was giving more and more time to Lewes FC, and busied myself writing and sending out press releases for activations I was organising. It's probably important to note that the club at this point had very strong ambition and vision, but very few staff to carry these out, so we were kind of laying out the train tracks as the train was hurtling towards us. The equality 'project' (this is what it was called on the board at first) was getting by on strong visionary words and actions from Ed and Charlie, and legwork from myself, spreading that vision out into the world. And so the nascent brand emerged.

Lewes FC Women's part-time marketing manager, Rosy Matheson, was also working on the development of the women's team, alongside a part-time women's general manager. Ed was finance director, Charlie was marketing director, and other directors led on facilities, operations and managing the men's side of the club, which was pretty much siloed off from the women's back then. A couple of female directors who had supported the equality project had either recently resigned or were about to. Directors were of course volunteers, and most had full-time jobs on top of the hands-on work they did for Lewes. The club was a labour of love and passion. Many volunteers helped with jobs around the ground and on matchdays, with the Supporters Club organising fundraising for, and carrying out, various maintenance tasks. Coaches were employed, but beyond that, there were hardly any paid staff. The club relied on its community to survive and grow, and though laudable, that is not necessarily a sustainable model for an organisation wanting to be exemplary on a world stage – so, much like any start-up company, we had to work hard and fast to bring revenues in and make equality work financially for Lewes FC.

Charlie had come up with a campaign called Unlock the Gate (supported by our local bus company and our independent cinema) to align with the suffrage-themed year of 2018 and attract more like-minded supporters to the club. The campaign would mark the hundredth anniversary of women in the UK first getting the vote, and use said anniversary to kick-start bigger crowds at women's football matches, asking individual women and women's groups to lead the way to the Dripping Pan. It would effectively use and expand on the networking and publicity I'd been doing. At that point we'd boosted the women's gate figure to an average of 250 fans at home games, which was small but the best in the FA Women's Premier League, as our league was then called. We wanted to reach 500 and beyond, and maybe one day sell out the stadium. These seemed like big dreams at the time.

We were keen to set an example that other clubs could follow and appeal to a whole new fan base of women who might not even like football but nevertheless wanted to support the efforts of female footballers to break through the thick glass ceiling that blocked them. And, of course, we also wanted to celebrate the amazing women (and men) whose courage had led to women getting the vote – the suffragettes. The plan was for the campaign to build up to Lewes FC Women's home game on 11 February, where we'd mark the hundred years since the Representation of the People Act unlocked the gate to (some) women finally being allowed to vote.

I'd been to WI meetings, Mumpreneurs gatherings and local school assemblies to tell the story of Equality FC to date. I'd talk about the history of the women's game, and invite kids and teachers and women to matches (under-16s have always gone free at Lewes matches, but are, of course, still counted on the gate[11]). We organised screenings of the film *Suffragette* at our

---

11 For the fair-minded and curious, canine fans aren't counted in the gate figure.

local cinema, and did short introductory talks on behalf of Lewes FC, linking the battle to get the vote with the battle for women to be valued in men's favourite sport. I also took advantage of the wonderful group of latter-day suffragettes who march at Bonfire every year for one of Lewes' famous Bonfire Societies (the Nevill Society), and asked if they'd consider doing the aforementioned flash mob with us, with a view to then marching to the women's match together. This being Lewes, they said yes.

Around this time, I received an email from the Soroptimists of East Grinstead. Once I'd worked out they were nothing to do with eye health, but rather a local branch of a huge global network seeking 'to educate, empower and enable opportunities for girls and women', I read on. One of their members had enjoyed an article I'd written in the *Observer* (on modelling, rather than football), and when they came across my name at Lewes FC, they thought I'd be an interesting speaker. In full-on activist mode, I thought, 'Right, I'm there.' All I needed to know at that point was that there would be a few people in the room who wanted to advance gender equality, and I wouldn't hesitate to say yes. But despite this strong sense of mission to introduce women to Lewes FC, as the time for the talk drew nearer, I was increasingly anxious. I think it was the idea of such a big audience; there would be 300 people at the event. Imposter syndrome? Well, no, because this was when I realised that for me, imposter syndrome was not so much a 'syndrome'; I really *was* a bit of an imposter in football. I decided that given what I knew so far of the game, this was probably no bad thing. I started to think carefully about my power as an outsider – the power to see things through an as yet unacclimatised lens and reassess. I rewrote my talk, this time concentrating on the pioneering suffragettes, who had aimed to 'wake up the nation' to an unacceptable status quo, as well as women's rights from a historical perspective. I put some slides together and got ready to present.

Not going to lie, it was lonely up there on stage, but as soon as I started with 'I've *never* liked football, but recently I've had my heart and mind changed by *women's* football – let me tell you why', I sensed the room perking up. Many of the audience could relate to the 'I've never liked football' bit, and there was a palpable interest in the 'women's football' bit. Since this was the year of the centenary of suffrage, and the overall theme of the evening was the suffragettes, it was a no-brainer for me to draw parallels between the famous suffragette slogan 'Deeds not words' and the decisive actions of Lewes FC in a sea of talk and passivity.

Calling for change via women's football was paramount to a sociocultural revolution, and that culture change was evident at the Dripping Pan, I promised the audience. Why were we the only club in the world not being sexist? Why were the FA scratching their heads about how to grow the women's game, how to get more girls playing, when the answer seemed obvious and simple – 'Clubs and governing bodies should stop putting all their money into men's budgets and put more resources behind women in football.' As the only club committed to equal playing budgets and resources, Lewes was leading the way in football, but it was hard work to make it viable, and we needed their support. We needed to sell more ownerships, more match tickets and attract more sponsorship. Whatever they could do to help us would contribute to transforming mindsets around the world. Lewes now had a global stage (it was true, we'd had unsolicited name checks and articles written about us in Austria, the US, France, Australia, Norway – the coverage was getting hard to track – and 15 per cent of our owners were in North America without us even targeting the area), and we wanted to set an example and be an inspiration for girls and women everywhere. All we needed was more people – them!

Later that same year, I was honoured with an 'Inspirational Woman' medal by the Soroptimists, having been nominated by Rosy. Audience feedback revealed that they 'hadn't expected to be interested in a talk about football', and yet they'd been inspired by it. This response was testimony to Ed and Charlie's determination (and weirdness), and I accepted the medal on behalf of the club.

With more talking gigs coming in, much as I wanted to spread the good news, I was nervous that I'd had no training in public speaking, and increasingly anxious, so I looked up a local confidence coach. Esther Egerton was an actor as well as a public speaking coach, and gave me a lesson on breathing and calming nerves. But the most important thing she said to me was, 'Remember, this is a performance.' Those words stay with me to this day, because, strangely, they released a lot of fear. This wasn't – despite the increasingly personal nature of some of my talks – about me. These were words I'd written about

Lewes FC that I needed to put across to an audience, a relaying of information in an engaging fashion, not a baring of my soul. Boom. I felt better! The more I understood that I was acting as a conduit for a greater purpose – in this case gender equality in football – the more emboldened I felt. I did try to talk more slowly, though. And to breathe.

As if to mark the end of that centenary of suffrage year, in December 2018, Lewes FC made history by playing a league match against the mighty Manchester United at the Pan. United had recently restarted a women's team and had entered the women's pyramid[12] at our league. Volunteers worked hard to pull off an amazing day, with everyone pitching in to welcome a sold-out crowd of 2,801 – our capacity at that time. The attendance set a record at the ground on what was a historic occasion. Matchday posters by Charlie that season featured inspirational women from the away team's locale, and so Lewesians saw the Mancunian suffragette founder Emmeline Pankhurst gracing shop and pub windows and coffee shop noticeboards all over town. Accordingly, and ever more emboldened by the mission, I used social media to find and invite her great-granddaughter – author and activist Helen Pankhurst – to come along as a guest of honour. Helen responded positively, and we went to town, featuring Emmeline in our matchday progcast (online programme for the match), and

---

12 The women's pyramid refers to the structured hierarchy of leagues for women playing competitive football in this country. There are fewer leagues at the top than the bottom, so it can be visualised like a pyramid.

organising a speaking slot for Helen before the match so that she could address the crowd on the subject of women's rights.

When I met her at the train station, Helen told me it was her first ever football match and that she'd become an owner of Lewes after my invitation because of the club's equality stance. After a pre-match rallying cry on the terraces, an exciting game, and book signings by Helen, we were interviewed by the BBC at full-time. Inspired by everything she'd seen and heard, Helen said, 'Football is important. It's feminism in action. It's about what women *do*, not what they look like. If Emmeline were alive today, she'd be right here at the Dripping Pan.'

We may have lost on the pitch that day against one of the richest clubs in the world, but our women played well; and I reckon Emmeline's great-granddaughter summed it all up very nicely.

Chapter 9
An Imposter Calls

———

It would do us all a bit of good if sometimes we tried to put
ourselves in the place of these young women . . .

J B Priestley

In April 2018, a posse of us from Lewes FC got ourselves on the
road to Wembley – to be interviewed for selection into the second
tier of English women's football.

Let me unpack that sentence a little.

As part of its drive to professionalise women's football,
the FA invited clubs to apply to be in what was previously
the Women's Super League 2 (WSL2) and would soon become
the FA Women's Championship (FAWC). The top league was
WSL1 and soon to become the Women's Super League, or *the*
Super League if you aren't into default male (exactly the kind
of unconscious diminishment I was *constantly* noting in football).

Charlie and Ed had already had some dealings with the
women's branch of the FA. Although they very much respected

the people involved, they had, of course, wound them up in the past. I say 'of course', because both are strong agitators who believe in equality, with all the assertiveness and privilege that comes with being straight white men (yes, you *can* use that privilege well!). Neither would ever take no for an answer (and yes, do imagine what this is like to live with), always having a comeback, always saying their piece, never letting the FA, or anyone else in football who sidelined women, off the hook. By contrast, the people in the Women's FA were part of a much larger organisation (the FA) and didn't have the freedom to implement equality immediately, even if it had been top of their wish list. Which was sometimes, and still is, debatable. What *is* clear, though, is that the Women's FA were on a mission to find clubs who could support, accommodate and finance elite women's football teams.

Lewes FC had employed a project manager to coordinate the completion of a long and detailed written application, as well as a presentation, because the club were taking this extremely seriously and knew that a promotion would be financially beneficial. The team for the day, tasked with persuading a panel of people to allow 'little' Lewes into the Championship (alongside Manchester United, Aston Villa, Crystal Palace and the rest), was Jackie Gilligan (director of operations); Glenda Thomas (application project manager); Ed Ramsden (financial director); John Donoghue (women's manager); Charlie Dobres (marketing director); and, well, me (always hard to pigeonhole into a role, it seemed).

I was asked along to talk specifically about my work with women's groups, and how we were changing fan culture at the Pan to include a market of previously 'unwelcome women'. I was grateful for the invitation, not least because it helped me to feel valued – I often felt a bit of an anomaly in the system, at home with the groups I was talking to but shyer among 'football people' who knew so much more than me. I was aware that my contribution would be to tell the kind of stories that the panel wouldn't have heard in their interviews with representatives from other clubs over the last few days. My work deliberately targeting other 'outsiders' and bringing them into the Pan, and so into football gave our club a competitive edge.

At a café near Wembley Stadium, the six of us ate sandwiches, gathering ourselves ahead of what we were all aware was a very important meeting for a relatively small club like Lewes, with the bigwigs of women's football. I felt a home advantage – we were after all in the familiar Borough of Brent, where I was born and bred! But the others were nervous, banking on this going well for the club's future and ambition for its women's side. I understood that a risk had been taken with Equality FC. We wanted to get to the Super League with our women, so that people might look at us, up against the female top guns of the Premier League clubs, and wonder, 'How on earth have *Lewes* done that?' And we would be able to say, 'Because of equality. Because we recognised sexism in football for what it is and did something about it.'

I was feeling supercharged, in fact, pumped up like a 'new face' on a model agency's books, ready to set foot on their first runway, or maybe an inexperienced striker making their debut on the pitch – nothing to lose, everything to gain. I relished the challenge of telling the panel about our football club, and the strong social purpose characterising it. We had everything in place to push the culture forward, using this game beloved by so many, and I was sure they'd see us for the advocates and doers that we were. Looking back, I now see that with the benefit of not belonging in football, I didn't quite appreciate the gravity of the situation. The others, now downing espressos with solemn faces and sweaty palms, clearly did. I didn't feel the kudos of the history of the place in the same way; the indubitable *honour* of being there. Nevertheless, this was a far cry from my feelings all those years ago when last at Wembley Stadium, watching England Men v USA Men, high up in the terraces among the beery blokes. Where was the challenge then? Where was the potential to change the world?

In the foyer downstairs, we took a commemorative photograph together, and looked at the visitors' book, noting that some of the clubs before us had sent just one or two people! Our six-strong group was surely a marker that we respected this process, that we knew we were punching, but that we were there to win. Apart from John and Jackie, who wore (very nice) tracksuits, we were all in our Sunday best (I'd dug out my smart Joseph coat, and Ed and Charlie, usually to be found in scruffy jeans or insouciant grey trackie bottoms, were fittingly suited and booted), reflecting just how much this opportunity mattered.

Upstairs, we were led through countless corridors – I noted the pictures of great *male* players and managers decorating the walls – to a grand corporate box with sweeping views of the famous pitch. It was impressive even to an interloper like me, whose dreams had never (in a million years) featured it!

In our box were seven or so interrogators from the women's FA, a mix of men and women. They seemed to be pleasant enough people, but their poker faces gave little away. Everyone around their shiny semicircular table looked stern, no doubt thinking hard about how to grow and professionalise the women's game, and whether Lewes were big enough and worthy enough to be part of that journey. Or maybe just wondering what on earth we were doing there.

Excellent presentations on the team, the club, our financial situation, stadium potential and marketing plan were confidently given by my expert teammates. And then I was asked about my work targeting traditionally 'unwelcome women' – a demographic likely not discussed by previous applicants. I smiled at everyone, saying hello again, before going into a consideration of how women could be treated as dehumanised sexual objects within a patriarchy, how we needed alternative role models to the ones we were constantly fed, and how I felt women's football *could and should* set an example in this. I continued despite some fairly blank faces. Not only would women be freed up by this dismantling of stereotypes, I persisted, but there would be a knock-on effect on men, who could choose to be vulnerable, emotionally expressive, and wear eyeliner if they wanted to, without having their masculinity questioned. Clearly, I suggested, the women's game was an opportunity to bring people together to champion each other in a united effort against stifling social conditioning. It represented a huge potential culture shift, did it not? Not just for the game of football, but for the whole of society to become more inclusive, more tolerant, to value women better.

I assured them that Lewes FC was rising to the challenge, appealing to women through off-pitch activations and alterations to the matchday experience. I may have alluded to the new Prosecco on tap flowing so well in the Rook Inn. I argued that our gate figures were proof that the concept of equality in football was a goer. I explained that I was, in business terms, a kind of 'customer zero', having deconstructed my opinion on football and become a huge fan of the women's game via the prospect of valuing female footballers equally to males. I saw now, I told them, that football was not 'a waste of time' but 'a game with huge power and influence'. I spoke directly from the heart, showing both my passion for change and my new-found enthusiasm for the women's game. I was quite glad my 15-year-old son wasn't listening in, because he would have either died of embarrassment or laughed his football-fact-stuffed head off. It's entirely possible I sounded like a weird religious convert.

I want to note here that working voluntarily for the football club, and at a stage in my life where I was privileged enough not to need payment to survive, meant that I was free to express myself with no regard for professional self-preservation. I was also very *willing* to express myself, because I believed that more people needed to know about women's football and the opportunities it presented. Hell, I'd even been trained for years to express myself honestly in various counselling groups! However, it seemed my personality was mismatched with football. The people across the table were looking at me, maybe a little stunned, one with a smile playing around her lips, one staring in apparent disbelief. One man appeared not to actually understand me, judging by his expression (although I was of course speaking plain English).

Football seems to have created for itself a slightly guarded culture, based on not disclosing very much; in fact, it seems to occupy a space at the other end of the communications spectrum from therapy. People in the business often struck me as a bit cagey or reticent, formulaic even. Managers and players in post-match interviews on the TV, for example, or typical club directors – they seemed given to cliché or formality. On the other hand, I'd always been open, and was of course unaffected by the cultural rules that seemed to govern the game. Therefore, I spoke freely, and without second-guessing what they might want to hear. I knew my message was valuable, because it was from an outsider to the game. I could see they had listened to me, but wasn't sure if I'd landed well. I did know I was ready to say it all again if asked. But I got only a slightly glazed silence and zero questions. I don't think they'd expected a diatribe on patriarchy.

'At the end of the day', though, as any good football manager might formulaically say, we did drive back down the M23 confident we'd given '110 per cent'. Course we did.

There followed a nervous wait back in Lewes, as we tried to manage our expectations. Would we get into the second tier? Were we being too audacious? Upstarts who should know our place? What were we even thinking?! But a month or so later? We found out that our application had been accepted. Little old Lewes would indeed be playing in the very same league as the likes of Manchester United, Aston Villa, Crystal Palace and Charlton. We would be, as of the 2018–19 season, one of the top 24 teams in the country. Ed and Charlie were ecstatic, and the little group of us gathered to celebrate as a team: a real coup for a club of our stature, we'd achieved a proper platform for our radical stance on equality. 'Here's to the future!' said Ed as we clinked our glasses together.

Lewes FC Women themselves were delighted too, of course, and very excited to prove their worth in the new league. John would look to strengthen the squad, and training hours would be increasing. This was a David v Goliath challenge we all believed we could rise to with quality football and a strong message.

Later that spring, Lewes striker Katie Rood and I were outside a pub in Brighton, having done a talk together, and got into a conversation with a group of friendly Brighton and Hove Albion supporters. As was my wont when out in public with one of our amazing female footballers, I proudly told them that Katie was a striker with Lewes and also played for New Zealand, waiting for impressed reactions. 'Oh yeah, Lewes!' they quipped. 'They just talked their way into the Championship, didn't they?!'

Roodie looked at them, then at me, smiling broadly – she knew the score. 'Yeah,' she answered. 'You know, maybe we just did.' We were proud Rooks!

As we moved into the Championship, and as more and more people responded to the messaging of Equality FC, so more and more turned up to our women's matches.

Chapter 10
Fan Engagement

Gird your loins or your uteri, and give me an 'L'!

Donna McPhail, Lewes FC Women fan,

former comedian, expert chanter

One day, I was at the Pan watching Lewes v Aston Villa with my friend the musician Jamie Freeman, who had recently become a proud owner. Like many men, he was very supportive of the women's team and completely backed Lewes' equality mission, having been turned off men's football himself because of 'the toxic, tribal atmosphere' – it wasn't just women who were unwelcome to football. Aston Villa (apparently nicknamed 'the Villans') had brought a very small but very loud group of male supporters, and a drum. They were chanting away and banging their drum and, by comparison, despite having many more fans, we had to agree that we were indeed 'like a library', as they gleefully sang. Apparently, as a fan, I was supposed to take offence at this, but instead I found it quite funny. Jamie didn't like it at all, though, and was adamant that we shouldn't stand for it, because 'This is our home!'

In football club lore, your 'home' is your home ground. It's not that you don't already have a home – you know, four walls, probably with a sofa, a fridge, a table, a bed, and maybe your nearest and dearest within – but this, this rectangle of perfectly manicured grass with stands around it and lovingly tended divots for the goalposts, turnstiles at the front, a clubhouse somewhere at the pitchside, this is yours. And it belongs to your fellow fans too. Together you protect and defend it, as well as inviting others to it for the afternoon. It contains a 'field of dreams', where battles are fought, lost and won, and cultures are formed, reputations built. It is your territory. Sometimes fans and players see it as their 'fortress'. I may be wrong, but I'm going to venture that this applies even more intensely to fan-owned clubs. Certainly, I'm now, at the time of writing, at the stage where if I see a Snickers wrapper on the floor, I pick it up. If I hear an away fan using homophobic language, I call them out. I wouldn't have it in my front room; I won't have it at the Dripping Pan.

So Jamie's concern informed my understanding of what the Dripping Pan symbolised. Or what it should, were I a fully-fledged fan. I was beginning to grasp his indignation. I knew what he meant by 'home', because I was also starting to understand the language. He witheringly called their drum 'a biscuit tin', which made me laugh. I was also understanding that although the fans were rude to each other, it was kind of expected, kind of funny – rudeness was allowed. Then he started to shout-sing, 'That's just a biscuit tin!' but with only one person singing, they didn't hear it across the length of the ground.

'You all need to learn to chant!' Jamie declared with some frustration, gesturing at me and a group of fan friends. We looked at each other, bemused, but clearly up for a new venture. 'Right,' he went on, pointing at me, 'Your kitchen, four p.m. next Saturday.'

Football chanting is one of those parts of fan culture that new female fans probably do have to learn. Unlike men, we're less likely to have been taken to matches by our dads, whereas young boys absorb the rules of terrace chanting almost by osmosis. Of course, some dads (and I've grown to call them 'dadvocates') take their daughters to football matches, and some mums do too, but back in 2018, before the Lionesses had conquered Europe, it was still rare. Certainly, my dad never had, and the idea of my mum taking me when I was young was just far-fetched – it was the park, the swimming pool or, if we were lucky, the cinema for us. So the thought of me and my pals standing around the perimeter of an oblong of grass and shouting out songs was, well, just a bit weird.

The following Saturday, Jamie gamely turned up at my house on his Vespa, where Rosy (from the club), Galia (my football-loving friend whom I'd encouraged to become a director because I thought the board needed more women), Lubna (a friend who had attended a few women's matches with me), Magnus (a gentle giant of a massage therapist who wasn't that into football but was into equality and game for a laugh) and I were already gathered, waiting for a lesson.

Together we racked our brains for chants that could involve 'the Rooks'. As mentioned, the club took its nickname from the grey-beaked corvids that nested in the surrounding streets, and the chess-piece-shaped castle on the hill. In much the same way, Brighton were the Seagulls, Sheffield United the Blades and Arsenal the Gunners. And us new supporters were realising that not only were the players the Rooks, but as fans we were sprouting black feathers too.

We thought we might help revive the existing chant, 'When the Rooks Go Marching In', but we would change the bit 'Oh when the Rooks shit on your car' to 'We are the Rooks from Lewes Town' – we were thinking about the families with young children who were starting to come along on Sundays to women's matches.

Jamie instructed us that everything must be sung three times, be 'anthemic' and, if possible, have a matching action (like an air punch at the end), ''cos them's the rules', he added. From there it wasn't long before we had fun with 'Rooks up*side* your head, I said Rooks upside your head', and then the ideas kept coming. In a moment of inspiration, Jamie hit gold with 'We will, we will *Rook* you', which we all felt verged on genius. We vowed to go to the next women's match together and get the crowd going.

Galia, Rosy and I met on the terraces and chanted together. We had some supportive friends around us who thought it was all a right laugh. Honestly? It didn't feel entirely natural at first, but we didn't let that get in the way of being fans. We sing-shouted at the top of our lungs – just a few of us that day – banging on the metal terrace bars with our ringed fingers for

'We Will Rook You'. Other fans looked at us, smiling. Maybe they laughed. I tried not to look too hard back, but I felt only support, no derision. Eventually a few kids joined in, taking to it like rooks to leftover chips, bless 'em, and it wasn't long before parents followed. It was all done slightly ironically, as a bit of a joke at first, but it caught on.

As we grew noisier, the atmosphere in the stadium became more buzzy, more rowdy. Not only were women's matches inclusive and welcoming, but now people were simultaneously laughing at the inventiveness of the chants and meaning them. We didn't know when parts of the crowd might erupt. It was a right giggle, and we were laughing at ourselves chanting as well as at the chants themselves.

I asked Donna McPhail – local Lewes fan and former comedian with a big voice – if she'd help lead the chants. A lifelong Sheffield United (men's) supporter, but now a massive fan of our women's team, she kindly stood in front of the terraces at a few matches to lead people new to the game in 'chanting practice' while I gave out song sheets, put together at her suggestion. It was an exciting time as we actively and intentionally changed culture. Donna would ask everyone to 'stand like a warrior' and reach their lower voice, gamely shouting, 'Gird your loins or your uteri, and give me an "L"!'

I was due to do a talk at Brighton Women's Centre's annual conference and asked if I could include a women's chanting workshop with Donna. They loved the quirky idea, because, well, who's ever attended one of those before? As my equality messaging and statistics on inequality in football were pretty heavy, and I'd been followed by our goalie Faye's experience of sexism hampering her progress, it was comic relief to have Donna introducing her bit with 'So the FA banned women because they were worried about our wombs, hey? And yet twenty-two guys running about with their reproductive organs flapping around on the outside is all well and good?' She showed a video of the New Zealand female rugby team's haka to get us warmed up. It worked. Fierceness was contagious, it seemed, and everyone stood strong and yelled 'We are the Rooks!' really loud, really feisty, really positive. It got riotous in there! I can honestly say I've never experienced anything quite like that group of women letting go and using their voices to shout for other women with such visceral conviction. The Lewes players, like Faye – who was standing there now, tough and strong, with a wide and incredulous smile on her face – had become such powerful symbols of the struggle to achieve gender equality. Every woman in the room was engaged, every woman empowered to shout out her determination for the Rooks to win. We'd found equality and we were taking it to church!

That summer (2019), Donna and I went to do the same thing together at a nearby festival, with me giving a talk on Equality FC before Donna spoke about the history of chanting at football matches, cracking us all up: 'And then there's "She fell over", a men's football chant directed at any player with long hair, or implying he plays like a girl – which wouldn't work for us at Lewes FC Women's matches, as it'd be a statement of fact. Also, we would all be going, "Yes, she did, didn't she? I hope she's all right."'

The other thing I remember about that festival is that we were billed in the programme as giving a 'chanting workshop', and quickly found out that half of our attendees were expecting a session on Buddhist chanting! It was a matter of a second's thought to present the idea of chanting to support other women as an expression of our mutual interdependence and bring on the positive vibes that resonated out into the universe when we chanted together at the Pan. We made some good noise in that tent: *everyone* was happy. At least some of the would-be Buddhist chanters joked on Twitter afterwards that they'd had 'a great, if unexpected' time.

Chanting continued at women's matches at the Pan, with the Men's Vets (over-35s recreational team) taking it up, supported by a couple of their members who were in the Lewes, Glynde and Beddingham Brass Band. 'Sussex by the Sea', 'We're the Red and Black Army', 'We Will Rook You', 'We Are the Rooks from Lewes Town', the *Match of the Day* theme, and 'Who Let the Rooks Out' (where we divided in half for a Q&A chant, and Benjy, someone's brown Labradoodle, often joined in), all became firm favourites on the terraces, with the Vets often starting the chanting, ably supported by all the girls and boys there for the football and the entertainment. Brilliantly, they transformed the traditional 'Yooouuu're shit! Aaarrrggghhh!' as the away goalie kicks the ball out (I'm still a little shocked by this ubiquitous chant when I go to men's matches, but the extra-aggressive echoing of 'aaarrrggghhh' all around the terraces is hilarious) to a more moderate 'Meeediocah, cah cah caaaaah!', which everyone agreed was a) very funny and b) very Lewes. I'd like to thank whoever gave their daughters signs at one match so that the home crowd knew what to say and when to say it, because those three girls running across the front of the home terrace behind the away goal with their handmade placards of 'meee', 'diocah' and 'cah cah cah' were nothing less than an utter stroke of genius.

Chapter 11
Talking the Talk

Find out who you are and do it on purpose.

Dolly Parton

With two full seasons of Equality FC under the club's belt, and the women's average gate figure quadrupling to 586, while the men's average gate had gone up by a couple of hundred too (to around 600), I was invited to speak to Brighton Chamber of Commerce members in March 2019 for International Women's Day.

This was a good opportunity because the networking meeting would be attended by local businesspeople (i.e., potential sponsors and owners), and it was in our biggest nearby city, with a population known for being inclusive, sustainably minded and, let's face it, progressive. We had yet to crack the Brighton market and were sure it was a potentially fab way to increase attendances – just ten minutes away by train, and then Lewes train station itself just two minutes' walk from the Pan. Easy. I was mindful not to diss Brighton and Hove Albion FC at any point for the fact that their women's team played in Crawley – miles away from the fan base – rather than at the Amex, BHAFC's main ground. Let's face it, it wasn't as if there weren't loads of other examples of this behaviour to give instead.

'You're not a bloke!' the young women who worked for the Chamber laughed at our pre-event meeting. We'd been chatting for about two hours – on those large, squeezy floor cushions that belong around outdoor swimming pools and (clearly) trendy workspaces – possibly without drawing breath. We all got on like a house on fire, talking about Brighton (such a friendly city), clothes (swapping vintage shopping tips), and the potential Lewes FC had to raise the self-esteem of young women like themselves who, right at that moment, didn't care much about football. We also chatted about the business networking potential of women's matches – what a great and so far largely untapped way for women in business to be introduced, chat to each other and form potential collaborations. Women's football matches could be like games of golf for men; we'd do deals on the terraces!

Their reactions made crystal clear to me a personal potential selling point: the incongruity between the way I presented and my subject matter. I went against all the stereotypical ideas they had at the time about people working in sport. I was interested in lots of stuff other than football – fashion, literature, make-up, music, art – and knew very little about the men's game. I never wore a tracksuit like many of my colleagues, in truth, largely for fear of accidentally setting the expectation that I *did* know something about the sport. As such, I appeared relatable, and these women were intrigued.

I was a human bridge between them and the big, bad world of football, which up until now had been fronted by men and shrouded in mysterious codes of language, culture and even danger.

Publicising the event beforehand in the local paper, one of them wrote: 'Karen Dobres was never ambivalent about football – in fact, she hated it. So how did she become actively involved in the beautiful game? A former model, manager and counsellor, Karen is not a typical football club press officer.' And quoted me as saying, 'It actually annoys me that we're having to battle for equality in football or any other business. To not be discriminated against for your innate characteristics is a basic human right, and I'm – carefully – angry about fighting for it. I'm looking forward to explaining why, given the opportunity, there is no reason women's football can't reach the same heights as men's.'

I meant it. And the women at the Chamber had specifically asked me to share not only what was going on at the club, but also my personal story of how I'd got into football. This made the event more nerve-racking than any talk to date. Previously players had shared their personal obstacles and journeys, but I'd concentrated on the history of women's football and the narrative of Equality FC at Lewes. Also, these people were *paying* to hear me talk. The apprehension kicked in. What if I'd be wasting their time and money? It wasn't going to be easy to look at an audience and tell them about myself, especially the relevant but awkward bits about having conformed to being a 'good girl' at school, the endless worrying about how I looked, being scared of football supporters, experiences of sexism, and then not even *knowing* women played football. I wished I was a bit cooler. Frankly, this was all potentially embarrassing stuff, but I'd have to get over myself.

On the morning of the talk, I chanted to calm my nerves (daily Buddhist practice rather than songs of the terraces, though they may also have worked, to be fair). I followed the commune with the universe with a practice run of the talk in front of Charlie, ending rather pathetically with 'I don't think I'm good enough.' My husband replied: 'No, you're not good enough. Now go and do it anyway. Go on, loser, just be yourself.' Understand, this was his way of *encouraging* me. And so I got on the train to cold, windy Brighton to talk to a sold-out audience about, yikes, Football and Me. And for the record, of *course* this 'be yourself' advice never works when it's the idea of being too much of yourself that makes your gut wrench! But, a true Brit perhaps, I liked the thought that I was a loser and not good enough. Nothing to live up to then. Aaaand . . . relax.

Arriving at the venue, I found the right room, noting that though *I* saw nobody I knew (bar the young women from the pre-event get-together), *they* all seemed to know each other, judging by the many absorbed conversations taking place. Looking back, this was probably small talk, which I've never been much good at (the trouble with coming from a therapy background – you either say too much deep stuff too quickly, or you hardly say anything at all because you're intensively listening and processing!). I also saw that they were mainly women. Good, I'd be free to relax even more without the audience feeling defensive or to blame – a phenomenon I'd noticed happening when I'd spoken to predominantly male groups. Here I realised I would be able to talk openly, mostly unencumbered by negotiating male feelings, i.e., reassuring them and being more mindful of their reactions, to enable them to carry on listening objectively. ('No one man here in this room is responsible for banning women from football, or for the patriarchy,' I'd say. And 'It's *not your fault!*' And 'We're all in this soup together!') It generally felt like more work the more men were present. And, frankly, work better accomplished by a bloke.[13]

Introduced by Andy Winter, the CEO of the event sponsor, Brighton Housing Trust, I performed – quietly at first, until I hit my stride – for about 45 minutes. I covered the usual – Equality FC, the history of the women's game, including the ban – but dwelled more on my own awakening to women's football at a time when I thought feminism was going backwards. During the noughties, when I was in my thirties, 'lad culture' had begun to thrive. It seemed to start ironically, but soon women were being over and over presented – on 'lads' mags' covers, in wet T-shirt competitions in university student unions – as one-dimensional objects existing to please men sexually. I explained my perception that we'd taken a downturn in terms of the way women and girls were seen in the world. And now it seemed that all over social media I saw women (not just celebrities, but influencers and . . . what would we call them? 'Normal'

13 Over the years, I've become educated better on talking about 'masculinity' as a changing, evolving concept, rather than about 'men'. It's helpful, if you *do* find yourself campaigning for gender equality in football, to see femininity and masculinity as constructs in this way (thanks, son, Alfie Dobres).

people?) emulating Bratz dolls, with artificially plumped lips, intense eyebrows, nails I can only describe as stressful, and entirely normalised cosmetic surgery. I'd reached a point where I was honestly worried about what young people thought girls were supposed to aspire to in the future. I related the existing reporting on the gender pay gap (of over 17 per cent in the UK in 2019) back to both the campaign for women to be allowed the vote in the early 20th century, and the battle for birth control in the sixties. All three of these were struggles that people had fought, or were fighting, just so that women might have agency within their own lives.

I talked about my own social conditioning, the restrictive beliefs I'd inhaled from child- and teen-hood, and the place I saw hope and experienced relief: the potential of women's footie to impact the world and change the way we all perceived women (and therefore men). I could feel my own anger about the pressure to be well behaved and modest when I was young, praised for being quiet, 'looking pretty', doing homework, caring for others; but never for being strong, or speaking out and up, making my own decisions, or for any kind of physical ability. I had done these (unpraiseworthy) things – either by the by, or against the odds – but they weren't what I'd learned to value myself for. I grew up independent in many ways, and risked being unappealing, going against the grain by taking time to swim regularly, leaving home aged eighteen to go to another country, and taking jobs wherever, but I never would have shouted about these things. Instead, I was constantly concerned that I should look 'attractive' to others, and be perceived as endearing, or at least polite.

'Ladette culture'[14] was slightly after my time and looked like fun, but I doubt I'd have joined in, as it was more important to fit in with the dominant narrative. Reading feminist books for the first time in my late teens opened my eyes a little, as did a male professor's hand on my leg in a university tutorial, and a photographer who would pester models to take off more and more garments on shoots, and later refused to book me unless I'd go out with him. I could *feel* the women in the audience relating to my gendered experiences as a girl and younger woman, and their interest piquing in the new subject of women's football.

I mentioned the critics of equality, and the kind of social media comments I (and Lewes FC Women on Twitter, which at that point was usually written by a bloke – Charlie, in fact!) provoked. They centred on the inferiority of the women's game. Here are some now (all from men), just for the lols.

'It's a niche sport in terms of viewing.'

'It is political correctness gone mad.'

'It's not "historical injustice" that women's football is absolute shite and nobody wants to watch it.'

---

14 The dictionary describes a 'ladette' as 'a young woman who drinks a lot of alcohol, uses rude language, and behaves in a noisy way'. The subculture emerged as a bid to break through from the confines of a more conservative form of femininity and freely exhibit behaviours usually reserved for young men.

'Women's football is slow, unattractive and often boring.'
'If some like it, great. Personally wouldn't watch it if they
where [sic] in my front garden. And I'm not sexist either.'

I warmly invited the audience to come down to the Dripping Pan and see whether they would experience a women's match in the way these male fans evidently did. I had my tongue in my cheek, but really, why were these men so self-important? Why did they assume that everyone would see things just as they did? Why did they mistake their opinions for absolute facts that would apply in any context? The answer seemed to be a particular kind of ignorance and male entitlement that can come with football – these guys simply didn't *need* to see that the whole system had been designed around men and that women had been routinely and deliberately edged out. Life and football simply hadn't required them to develop the empathy to conceive of another point of view. The way they made their points was far more interesting than the points themselves. Which, let's face it, were pretty rubbish.

After my part was over, Andy introduced the Q&A, saying this was one of the most inspirational presentations he had heard and that he was going to become a Lewes FC owner immediately. (He did, and has been a vocal supporter of the club on and off the terraces ever since, once giving me a large green vuvuzela that absolutely no one else at Lewes FC thanked him for. Thank you, Andy.) There were questions about the practical steps taken to enable equality, what should people expect when they came to a match, and . . . what was it like to be a model? My answers were about vision, board structure and activation, Prosecco on tap and friendliness, and the weirdness (and fun!) of the world of fashion and image. Afterwards an actual queue of people formed, all asking to become owners of Lewes FC. I'd told them the absolute truth: that buying a share in a football club was in fact less expensive than buying a good tub of face moisturiser – a bargain in other words – and would likely do more to keep your face smooth than retinol if it made the world more equal for women! People were laughing at themselves – agreeing that owning a football club had before this morning not been any kind of consideration in their lives, but now . . . well, it felt like most of the room wanted in!

At that event, I witnessed the power of a personal narrative of realisation to help people reach a deeper understanding of the impact this football club could have in changing an entire culture, and their potential part in it. Each time I convinced an audience, their reactions made me reconvince myself! This was one room of people. What if we could reach audiences of far more?

There were often social media write-ups after talks, so I have quotes from various – often slightly stunned – women.

'Never thought I'd see the day when I felt inspired and excited by FOOTBALL! I've never been a follower of spectator sports, and never been super capable AT sports, but I left the Brighton Chamber event this morning considering going to see and buying a share in Lewes FC as soon as possible!'

'Literally about to go and join Lewes FC and attend my
second ever football match.'
'Women's football was banned? *What the living chuff?!*
Joining Lewes FC as an owner today.'

I enjoyed this role I'd dropped into. Enjoyed using my own
new experience of this product – women's football – and the
insights it had given me to accelerate the take-up among fellow
women. Loved that women were spending their money on Lewes
FC's bid to change the world by properly valuing themselves as
equal to men, and that we weren't talking about the kind of things
advertisers were always shoving in *my* face: I'm thinking expensive
'age repair cream', feminine hygiene products, 'tweakments',
bikini-body workouts and wrinkle-erasing silicone patches. We
were all flipping the bird to the Establishment. If more women
owned football clubs, we might even change those undermining
pesky algorithms. I'm convinced we'd all have fewer wrinkles.

Armed with business cards from women in their twenties,
thirties, forties, fifties and sixties, I made the ten-minute train
journey back to Lewes clear that we needed to change the system
to accommodate people like us, rather than change such people
to fit in with the system. This strong intention to disrupt the
status quo would become part of a growing ambition to change
the world through football. Board members messaged me that
they'd had lots of ownership sign-ups, and could I please keep
doing whatever I was doing.

Chapter 12
Stirring the Cup

———

A woman must have money and a pitch of her own if she is to
play football professionally.

Me, with thanks to Virginia Woolf

(*A Room of One's Own*)

It's a funny thing, but if we're talking about radical ideas, I should
mention that just a couple of miles down the road from Lewes
FC, in the village of Rodmell, lived the author Virginia Woolf.
Woolf was a nonconformist. Her famous book *A Room of One's
Own* once gave me the answer to an annoying question asked by
a male cousin.

At university I studied English literature. I grew to love Milton,
Shakespeare, Chaucer, Hardy, Dickens, Owen, Auden and the rest,
but the shared gender of all these wonderful, skilled and assured
wordsmiths had never occurred to me. A bit like the female players
who had grown up football-crazy with posters of male football
heroes on their bedroom walls, my bookshelves as a teenager and

a young woman heaved under the weight of male authorship, and I'd never really noticed. Nosing about my university room while on a visit, my cousin Clive asked me why all my books were written by men. I was a little shocked, maybe a little shamed (being not male myself) when the fact was pointed out to me, and aggrieved to have no immediate response to it. Did he think women couldn't be good writers? Did *I* now momentarily think women couldn't be good writers? I think I stuttered something along the lines of 'Well, of course, women weren't educated like men were, and probably couldn't read and write unless they were from the upper classes. What was the point in teaching them when their work involved child-rearing, cooking, cleaning and maybe, I don't know, some light farming on the side?' I was aware that the Brontës – vicar's daughters – had had to write in book margins (no paper), and Jane Austen in crowded parlours as she didn't have, despite relative class privilege, – you guessed it – a room of her own. I also knew that the Brontë sisters were forced to use male pseudonyms at first, just to get published, and that the great novelist George Eliot was a woman who, out of necessity if she wanted her work read, adopted a man's name. But I'd never thought about it properly – too busy trying to translate *Beowulf*, analyse *Coriolanus* or make sense of Joyce, while being grateful that I was even at university. So well done, Clive, for exposing the wallpaper!

It wasn't until I read Woolf's illuminating book – an account of two speeches she made on women and fiction – that a heavy penny dropped. Woolf surmises that if Shakespeare's sister had tried to write professionally, she would probably have been raped trying to get to London, died early, or been worn out and impoverished from unwanted child-rearing and the business of survival before she'd had a chance to get hold of a quill and a bit of parchment, let alone get anything performed. A veil was lifted for me as I digested the words. As she wrote, Woolf's mind wandered from her life as a woman to those of other women, from libraries to kitchens, conjuring up women's collective past (and in some parts of the world the conditions she describes are still very present). It's an absorbing and profound book on how far, in Woolf's time, we had and hadn't progressed. She sets out the precarious life of a historical woman who will for ever be anonymous, and her imaginary account explains why Shakespeare's sister's talent and determination would not have got her anywhere in a system designed only for her brother's literary success. (On a side note, I named one of our floodlights at the Dripping Pan after Virginia Woolf as a crowdfunder prize. Just as the author shone a light on one male bastion, now she shines one on another. And on another side note, Shakespeare did indeed have four sisters, but two died, and the others are, guess what, not famous.)

This conversation with Clive and reading *A Room of One's Own* steered me to look more into the world of feminism and language, and I began noticing all the times 'he' was used in supposedly gender-neutral books, and how when I read the words 'author' or 'director' or 'boss', in my head I was inevitably imagining a man. If you think about it, it's a bit of an issue when you're a young woman with a – hopefully interesting – future to envision.

And now here I was, many years later, in football. When I heard 'footballer' or 'football fan', or 'referee', or certainly 'football club director', I pictured a man. It was clearer to me than ever that women were not really part of the dominant narrative. I saw that they didn't have pitches to call their own. I saw how under-resourced females were in football. I saw that talented female players emerged despite, and not because of, the system. I saw how the structures of football were designed for men, and I started to wonder. About the pictures of the great Bobby Moore, for instance, that I'd seen in the women's loos while at Wembley Stadium. I wondered why there weren't any female players above the hand dryers. I wondered if the much-admired Bobby had had a sister. Had she ever been into football? I wondered whether she'd had encouraging parents back in the sixties while women were still banned here. (Interestingly, Lewes FC Women's captain at the time of writing, the popular Rhian Cleverly, has a twin brother who was encouraged to play football, while her parents wanted her to do ballet. Her brother's now an actor, and *she's* the pro footballer.) Would Bobby's sister have had enthusiastic coaches or teachers? Would she have found girls to play with? Would she have had any female role models to look up to and build her hopes and dreams around? Yes, I know it wasn't women who beat Germany in 1966 – but the question is, *why* wasn't it? And I think we know the answer. No disrespect to either William Shakespeare or Bobby Moore intended here, by the way, just spitting facts and ruminating on a male privilege I'd not seen properly acknowledged before.

So, how to change this system where men seemed to have all the interesting, meaty jobs and women the supporting or decorative roles? Woolf had identified money and space (i.e., resources) as being the key obstacles for women writing fiction, who would, inevitably, write from the female perspective, reflecting an alternative reality. It was the same in football. How to resource women and give them a level playing field in a game so cruelly snatched from them in 1921? How to let them develop their own game? Charlie and Ed saw an obvious and karmically appealing answer: equalisation of the FA Cup prize fund.

The FA Cup is the flagship competition of football's governing body in England. It's a cup that teams up and down the country dream of winning, and works according to knockout rounds that normally see the richest clubs triumphing. Of course, there are wonderful and memorable anomalies in which smaller clubs play bigger clubs and David-and-Goliath situations emerge, taking fans on journeys of the heart, soul, train and motorway. The FA Cup itself is still default male, so there is also the *women's* FA Cup. But as I'm talking about Lewes' women's team, I'll do us all a favour and refer just to the FA Cup (enough of that default male – too deceiving and insidious).

Charlie and Ed proposed that the FA Cup should have attached to it exactly the same prize fund as the men's FA Cup. A bold proposal maybe, given the kind of money we were talking about, but I suspect Virginia Woolf would have been all for it.

As it stood, that season (2018–19), Lewes FC Women were performing well in the FA Cup and due to play Arsenal away in the fourth round in March. So, once again using our football journey as a vehicle for social change, Charlie and Ed drafted an open letter, approved by the board, to the FA. It highlighted some of the vast gender-based disparities that existed at every stage of the cup fund. Disparities like the winning men's team getting £3.6 million and the winning women's team getting £25K. Or like the total prize fund for the losing men in the first two rounds being more than the total prize money paid to women in the whole of the competition including the final. Or that the total prize money for women was, in fact, less than 1 per cent of the total prize money for men.

The letter referred to itself as a 'healthy challenge' to the FA. At this point in time, the FA had declared that it was attempting culture change by growing and professionalising the women's game, so the letter constructively suggested it could help them do this. It also drew attention to how much money it cost clubs for women's teams to play in the elite levels of football.

So it was that in February 2019, Lewes midfielder Shannon Moloney stood in the club's echoey old home changing rooms (good acoustics) and read the letter aloud as Charlie and I filmed her. 'The FA Cup provides an ideal mechanism for financially irrigating the women's game,' she said, and put forward Lewes FC's proposal for a 'radical increase in the women's prize fund'. 'What a story it would be,' she emoted to camera, 'for the world's most beloved domestic cup competition to become the Holy Grail that champions women's football into a whole new era!'

The disparities were huge and shocking, of course. The numbers themselves spoke volumes, and our letter and campaign made headlines once again. 'Lewes call on FA board to look at gap in prize money in men's and women's competitions,' said the BBC. 'Football Association under pressure to increase women's FA Cup prize money,' declared the *Telegraph*, while the *Guardian* led with a quote from Lewes FC Women: 'We've earned £45,000 for the club but for men it would have been £450,000.'

When the Rooks played the mighty Arsenal in our televised cup match in 2019, we fans wore T-shirts boldly proclaiming what we stood to win in the fourth round, and the men's equivalent prize in the same round (£360,000 for the men, £3,000 for the women). The facts looked bad when laid bare for all to see. And wasn't this flagship competition surely the perfect opportunity for the FA to make reparations for the ban all those years ago – the consequences of which had likely brought us to where we were right now, with the women's game dragging so far behind the men's?

However, Arsenal knocked us out and campaigning was put on hold until the next opportunity, which, due to 2020's pandemic, would be in the 2021–2 season. By this time, the FA had indeed increased the women's total prize fund – a hundred years after they'd banned the game – to £309,000. But the men's total prize fund had also been increased, and was now some £16 million, so in effect widening the gap! You couldn't make it up, could you?

Comparing matches played in the equivalent rounds of the women's and men's competition, a men's team winning their first-round match in the 2021–2 season took home £16,972.

A women's team winning in the same round were laughing all the way to the bank too, until they looked at the cheque: £850 (and no, there are no zeroes missing). Just for *losing* in that same round, a men's team got £5,657. It gets worse. By the time the final was played, the winning men's team pocketed a rather lovely £1.8 million – even the loser of that match received £900,000. Want to guess the riches with which the winning women's team was lavished? It was £25,000.

The club responded with something different.

This time, Charlie proposed a fairer FA Cup for all, including lower-league men's teams. The new proposal would stop the usual Premier League clubs gobbling up all the prize money (where it frankly would make very little difference) and redistribute the funds down the men's pyramid and into the women's game, where it would be *transformative*. Under the proposed distribution, men's and women's teams would receive the same prize per fixture, but the prize would be weighted to increase as teams progressed through later Cup rounds. The men's total prize fund would initially be larger, as there are currently more teams in their Cup – at least until women's football grows in popularity and more teams enter. Crucially, however, the prize per fixture would not be calculated based on sex. To this day, Charlie's calculator is on the website, where you can type in the name of your club and see how much better off they'd be under the new system (unless your club is in the Premier League, in which case they really won't suffer!).

In 2022, when Lewes FC Women drew Manchester United in the quarter-finals of the FA Cup, the players, inspired by the club's campaigning, composed a second letter of their own asking the FA for a more equal prize fund. They wore shirts illustrating once again the vast disparity that still exists.

As I write this book now (October 2024), Lewes are preparing to play Dulwich Hamlet in the first-round proper of the Cup. If they win, they will get £6,000, whereas men's team winners at the same stage of the competition would get £45,000. To put it into perspective, a £45,000 win for a club like Lewes is the difference between having a communications manager and not having anyone officially doing communications apart from volunteers and other staff chipping in. Even the male losers in this first round will get more than double what the women winners will get, at £15,000. The overall winners of the women's FA Cup will get £450,000, whereas the male winners will get £4 million. By 2024, however, the campaigning was at least starting to work, and the total prize fund for the Women's FA Cup stood at nearly £6 million, with much of it going to smaller clubs in the early stages of the competition, as we'd asked for. But – and in gender equality, there's always a but – the gap between the women's and men's prize fund still stood at a whopping £14 million. The campaigning continues to this day, largely taken up by players.

Sometimes you have to show the system up.

I want to draw attention to the fact (in case it's useful for changing other male bastions) that Charlie and Ed – two men – led on this proposal. Both were fully aware of the facts around the FA Cup prize fund and disgusted by the male bias. I think it's significant that those with the power (men in football) led on change for the group with far less power (women in football). To make effective change, we need the dominant group to activate, supported by the less powerful group, who can feed them information via their less privileged lens. This is how activism seems to work best in a world set-up for the dominant group to have more impact, more confidence, more swag.

As another example, this time where I held some power due to my skin colour, I remember being invited to a law firm's office for a breakfast at which the subject of inclusion was to be discussed. I was asked along because the firm were considering sponsoring Lewes FC in order to align with our undeniably practical demonstration of how to include women in a traditionally male space. Current and potential sponsees as well as high-ranking representatives from major clients were on the guest list. As I walked through the door, I was offered tea by a young black woman. Scouting the room, I noted that she was the only black person there; everyone else was white or brown. We swapped pleasantries and inside shopping information about our clothes, establishing a friendly, supportive connection that way. She was a junior assistant to a white male lawyer, and I sat between her and her boss in the room we were led to. We were there to give our experiences and talk about inclusion, following a presentation on the subject from a legal point of view.

At some point during the meeting, a white woman from a major charity mentioned the Black Lives Matter movement, criticising it for not including 'all lives'. I was flabbergasted and wondered who was going to challenge this statement to explain why the movement focuses specifically on black lives. Too many seconds passed while no one said a word. I shifted in my seat, feeling adrenaline rise in my system. Acutely conscious that it wasn't the one black woman's responsibility to speak out against a white client, I used my unearned but evident privilege as well as my challenging but character-building experiences at Lewes FC to speak out. I explained to the woman from the charity why the movement wasn't about all lives, but about those affected so tragically by our racist systems and mentalities. I added – still internally taken aback that I was even *having* to explain – that this didn't discount the value of other lives, but gave us a focus for change, one that we obviously very much needed. Coming from another white woman, I believe this was more effective – not to mention less triggering – than if the young black woman had had to explain. I like to think that anyone connected with Lewes FC would have done the same. My experience at the club has taught me that we're never going to change the world by either keeping quiet or relying on other people. And we certainly won't do it by asking women to step up to change gender inequality, or black people to solve racism.

Around the same time as our initial open letter to the FA about the FA Cup prize fund, Shannon Moloney and I were invited to Parliament, to the APPG (All-Party Parliamentary Group) for Sport, Modern Slavery and Human Rights. Here we were asked to speak, alongside others, for eight minutes each on discrimination in football. We were to consider what the obstacles were to full collaboration from federations who should have an interest; the importance and role of governance in this issue; our call to action; and finally, to whom it was addressed.

Shaz and I were excited and nervous, and as was often the way when I hung out with female players, she taught me a good lesson that day. We met outside a London tube station, where Shannon shared a selfie for her Instagram story saying, 'Off to Parliament!' She told her many followers that she had her 'Game Face On!' I realised, delighted, that she was approaching the event as she would a football match. She wore full make-up, her hair was done, and, more important than any of that, she had the most brilliant, determined smile on her face – we were going to Parliament to *win*! Since that day, whenever I'm attending an important meeting or an event and I put my lippy on, I tell myself I'm getting my game face on, and imagine a team of women behind me who have my back. Not only does it put me in 'fighting mode'; the imaginary team of female warriors at my back shore me up and really do make the dream work.

At the session, I delivered a rallying cry (written with Ed and Charlie) from Lewes FC about the need to resource the women's game and publicise its history, while Shannon gave them an emotional rendition of her playing career before being signed by Lewes. I don't believe anyone round that table will ever forget the story of Shannon's socks, least of all the wonderful chair, over-60s footballer and member of the House of Lords Baroness Lola Young, who subsequently became an owner of Lewes FC.

Chapter 13
A Seat at the Table

You're gonna be doing your own head in every time you go to
work if you don't keep telling yourself you're a man.

Sinéad O'Connor

Shortly after this, in July 2019, and much to the surprise of
my parents, friends, cousins, uncles, aunts, etc., what felt
like the inevitable happened and I joined the board of Lewes
FC. The directors had agreed, in a meeting where Charlie
had, quite rightly, left the room and not been able to vote,
that I should be co-opted to bring my experience to the board,
and continue to work on the new market of fans for the women's
team.

Mum: Are you sure, dear? The kids need you.
Friend 1: *Random*, but well done. Let's do coffee.
But. Please. Can we not talk about football?

Friend 2: That's *so* weird! Have you finally lost it? You *never* have any time any more at weekends. And no, I don't wanna come to the match.

Male cousin: Hahahahahaha.

Son: (ironically) Not *more* feminism, OMG.

Daughter: Nope. Still not coming to a football match.

But my loved ones could no longer pass this 'football' obsession off as a strange choice of performative foolishness, or an obsessive mid-life crisis, because shit – as they say – was getting real.

My sister, Jane, came along to a talk I did in the wine cellar of a London hotel, and finally forgave me for missing my niece's primary school singing debut in favour of a Lewes FC Women match. Afterwards, she WhatsApped, *Loving this fresh perspective on boring old football! You nutcase.* It was great to have her support. I'm sad to this day about missing my niece's performance, though.

My mum came to her first match ever with me, insisting on joining in by shouting, 'Kick it, kick it!' to the women on the pitch. That felt slightly less supportive, but I nevertheless appreciated her effort.

A group of my local Buddhist friends came to watch a game, inspired by my social media ravings about Lewes FC Women. I felt guilty because it was a particularly cold Sunday in winter, and no number of blankets – they'd come prepared – could quite stop them from freezing on the terraces!

Being on the board lent added authority to the work I continued to do amplifying Lewes FC's message to not only the new market of 'unwelcome women', but also potential sponsors. By now, apart from the talks and media interviews, I'd written to CEOs of multinationals, getting warm responses and commercial meetings, as well as organising free gym membership and yoga instruction for players at a local health club, plus donated yoga mats from another multinational, and various other local collaborations. It would be fair to say I was truly obsessed. Utterly convinced of the shared value Lewes FC could offer to any business by sprinkling the fairy dust of brand alignment, I made it part of my day to fire off an email each evening, getting familiar with RocketReach, a website that gives you potential email addresses.

For some weeks I was enthralled with the idea of Chanel's Rouge Noir nail varnish sponsoring the club. I learned the story of its invention (they'd been running out of classic red behind the scenes at a show and experimented with a black-red mix to make the red last longer. Bingo! It became a bestseller). Faye said she'd wear it under her goalie gloves. Like a witch casting a spell, I painted my own nails ebony-red and used those fingers to type emails to Chanel's marketeers. I didn't understand when they turned me down. So I wrote to the CEO of Unilever, as he had publicly stated that he wanted all his brands to become 'purpose-driven', and he promptly – and to the rest of the board's surprise, as they hadn't expected a response – set me up with Dove.

Frustratingly, despite a great meeting, they said they were a beauty brand and needed to focus on appearance-related issues. But this *was* about beauty. To my mind women's football and equality in football *were* definitely in part an appearance-related issue – it platformed a different way of being beautiful. I approached other brands, but it wasn't easy to convince those holding purse strings of the new representation of the feminine that I loved so much. Were we not still the only football club who made it our business *not* to write off 51 per cent of the population? Was football not a massive opportunity to have conversations with men about gender equality? To speak to women about looking good on their own terms, rather than for anyone else? Didn't absolutely everybody need to help lead the way to changing the world via this platform? We were offering a way to support people breaking free of restrictive gender stereotyping, and in a nutshell, once we'd empowered women, and given men the chance to be vulnerable and 'feminine', we would all get along better and achieve great things. In short, I was unswervable, and, let's face it, probably an insufferable bore to my nearest and dearest.

Apart from Charlie, of course, who was just as into it. Can you imagine the endless conversations in our kitchen over dinner? In bed first thing in the morning, before we'd even put the kettle on? On car journeys? I don't know why we were like this, but all I can say is that there is probably something wrong with us both, and that is why we get along.

I was inspired by the words of Franklin Thomas, the American businessman and philanthropist, and had his quote Blu-Tacked to my wall in between matchday posters, poetry excerpts and Buddhist sayings: 'If the struggle of the last decades was against the colonialism that allowed one nation to rule another, the current and future struggle will be about the internal colonialism that allows one race or sex to dominate another. One day our descendants will think it incredible that we paid so much attention to things like the amount of melanin in our skin or the shape of our eyes or our gender, instead of the unique identities of each of us as complex human beings.'

I was both excited and nervous before my first board meeting. It started at 6.30 p.m. and went on until gone 10. In July 2019, this length of time for the fortnightly meetings was both typical and necessary. They were held in either the Rook Inn (clubhouse) or the Portakabin (coaches' offices and hospitality area) at the club, and there were usually eight to ten board members present. At the point when I joined, there were two other women on the board. One was my friend Galia, whom I'd encouraged to join because she was a woman in business *and* has always liked football, with a fine tale of once massaging John Barnes' shoulders on an aeroplane. Galia was running her own company, and found the amount of communication on the directors' online channels overwhelming and too time-consuming (tons of time was needed from board members at this point due to not having enough operational staff). Sadly, she stepped down before her term was up. She told me she had felt excluded from some footballing discussions by not always being informed of when meetings were happening, as well as not being able to make them. And there was Michelle, a scientist friend of Ed's, who was keen to help but, living in London with two small children, also found the amount of time involved ultimately too much. She stepped down after a few months.

I was in the useful position of living locally, knowing Charlie and Ed very well, having independent children, no regular, demanding job, and being familiar with a couple of the other directors. In other words, I was well supported by some of my male colleagues, and came to understand that I would need every ounce of this support to stay in position. Mary Beard, author of *Women & Power*, said, 'You can't easily fit women into a structure that is already coded as male, you have to change the structure,' and this was a case of working within a system that was coded male, and which most of the men who inhabited it seemed blind to. There were cultural passwords like 'What was the score last night?' and everyone else knew which particular match – whether it was national, international or the Lewes Boys under-18s – was being referred to and, well, the score. They knew the score. There were unspoken rules and conventions that simply didn't figure in my frame of reference, and which I was surprised to rub up against. I *didn't* know the score, you see. As a kind of Alice figure, the first alien code of behaviour I encountered at this tea party in Wonderland was that *no one approached the kettle* . . .

The directors present at my first meeting were all men, sitting around a large table in our utilitarian Portakabin. Apart from male faces, the first thing I saw was that there was a kettle, tea bags, coffee, sugar, milk and stained mugs on a side table, and yet no one round the table had a drink. I knew *I'd* like a cup of tea, so I asked if anyone else would. Making the tea was something

I was trained to do in childhood. And my mother would *never* allow my sister or me to get a cup of tea just for ourselves if there were other people around – unthinkable. Imagine that! A woman selfishly putting herself first when there were others, especially *male* others, who might be in need!

Everyone in the Portakabin answered affirmatively, saying they'd have black coffee, or tea with two sugars, or a touch of milk ('but not too much, don't give me gnat's piss'), etc. And that, my friends, is how I found myself spending the first ten minutes of my inaugural board meeting making tea and coffee for a large group of men and missing the first agenda item! Nobody thought to get up and help me, and nor did I have the wits about me to ask them to.

This is what can happen when a system is coded male (they don't think about making tea) and you are female, but you nevertheless want to be yourself. I learned pretty quickly that I shouldn't be *fully* myself or I'd miss the actual business! My learning was to *stay away from the kettle*. No matter how magnetic it sometimes seemed – and believe me, kettles *are* like magnets to someone who's been brought up to offer everyone who comes through the door a cup of tea *and* a sandwich – I never approached it at a board meeting again. As the artist Sinéad O'Connor said in her book *Rememberings*, about her life in the music industry (yet another male bastion, of course), 'You're gonna be doing your own head in every time you go to work if you don't keep telling yourself you're a man.'

Sometimes I thought I did need to 'ape' men a little, especially while initially getting involved in this existing system. But then when a new female board member, or any person from a marginalised group, finds all the ways in which the system doesn't really fit or makes them uncomfortable, they question and reimagine that culture. If they are in a position to change behaviours and policies, then more diverse folk are in turn attracted. And then we might even see a change in culture when it comes to the details like, I dunno, making the tea! I don't need to ask if I'm right, because the experience of my first seven years at Lewes FC has shown me that this is how it works, in football at least. It is why we need more diverse boards and more diverse experience in those decision-making roles. I'll tell you some more things I did soon – far away from kettles – and they will make you cringe and possibly smile. But for all the smiling, we have to recognise the seriousness of diversity, both for business and for all of us as human beings.

Just prior to joining the board, I'd attended a talk by Caroline Criado Perez about her book *Invisible Women: Exposing Data Bias in a World Designed for Men*. She was eloquent on patriarchy and the 'one size fits all' approach that was endangering women's lives, never mind our confidence. I asked her what the answer was to this pervasive problem of a systemic bias that sees products, services and systems designed based on data that disproportionately represents men. Caroline thought hard. Then she said, 'We need to make the feminine aspirational.' Well, I thought, that's exactly what we're trying to do at Lewes FC with women's football – to value it more highly, and market those women as the role models they are, according to their own values! So, from then on, I decided to be as much myself – as in true to my experience, personality and principles – as I could possibly be on the board. Being myself was, in itself, radical. I kept telling myself I was a good addition, despite my lack of footballing expertise and my gender. In fact, I'd argue that I was a good addition *because* of this. I knew I was on the back foot in terms of football and had a lot to learn, so made it my business to ask questions when I didn't understand something. Also, after that first meeting, I made sure to bring my own flask of tea!

In October of that year, I stood for election to the board, and became a director with voting power. Another step change. As an elected custodian, I now felt a responsibility towards the *whole* club, not just the women's team. And so began another eventful period of unexpected collaborations coupled with obstacles. I decided to attend men's matches as well as women's, as I now felt it was right to do so. These matches were to be a real eye-opener as it finally dawned on me that men's football wasn't just about the top leagues, which I'd been used to seeing on TV or in the papers. Football really wasn't just . . . football.

One of the first things I did on the board was formalise connections made through my talks to women's organisations. I asked my contacts at groups like Lewes Women in Business, the Soroptimists, the Mumpreneurs, Survivors' Network and Brighton Women's Centre if they'd like to form an official group called Lewes FC's SisterShips. The SisterShips became a growing network that empowered girls and/or women in some way, that supported Lewes FC's equality initiative and that the club mutually supported in return. Other members included Rise, a domestic abuse charity based in Brighton; Sussex Police's

'HeForShe' campaign; Brighton's Co-Women Network; Active Sussex; the Girls' Network and Lewes Women in Art. The aim was to offer them discounted tickets for women's matches, both raising the gate figures and encouraging the groups to network in the physical space of a women's match. Many of the women in the SisterShips were, like me, not (yet) fans of football. We launched at a women's match, and this innovation continued for some years, enhancing the club's standing in our community, bringing in revenue and gathering our target audience of women and girls for women's matches.

There are, of course, many wonderful groups of women promoting feminism and gender equality, but I felt I was making best use of the time – and my director gig was to take up at least a few hours every day, including weekends and some evenings, for a further three years – promoting gender equality with, among and to *men*. Just as racism is a problem white people need to be galvanised to respond to, so gender inequality is a problem men need to be aware of and address. For women to take their rightful place in football, it's helpful for men to understand what their male football privilege bequeaths them so easily, without them having to do a thing to earn it. And, ideally, to understand a little bit of what it's like not to have that privilege – emotionally and practically. And then – and this is the big one – it's bloody amazing when it becomes clear that by helping to bring about more equal conditions, men actually benefit too. Like the men's gate figure rising after the club created a level playing field for women. We all have gender-associated gifts, ideas and ways of working that, given half a chance, can be mutually helpful.

Writing this down, it's scarily apparent that the task I envisioned ahead was no easy one, and that doing it – while co-creating and facilitating the strategic direction of a football club, as well as helping run it day to day – was going to be a challenge. One that involved both personal and institutional change. I was ready to change as a person – indeed, I already had, thanks to the female footballers – and felt vicariously empowered by their exploits on the pitch. Moreover, my experiences waking up the new market continued to give me more confidence in my own values, abilities and story as a human being. But was everyone else on board, and did they need to be?

It was a question that kept pinging in my head during my first few board meetings, and I remain deeply interested in it to this day. Prior to being on the board, I had only really dealt with Ed and Charlie – the two directors who had staked their elected places on the introduction of gender equality and were constantly discussing the club's future in those terms. I'd call them both feminists, and I think they would too. One was my husband, and the other observed 'Bloomsday' every year to celebrate James Joyce's novel *Ulysses*, and insisted that Lewes FC's teams wished all their followers a happy Bloomsday too – which was enough for me to know that I could rely on Ed as a forward-thinking agent of change, unafraid of doing things differently. But here on the board, meetings were taken up with long discussions on subjects such as toilets (very necessary, of course), relationships with men's managers, matchday logistics, marketing and organisation. Some of the male board members seemed to me to be a little unresolved, or at least less interested, around the gender equality messaging and activations. Some were only there for the football (I got that – this *was* the board of a football club) and seemed most motivated by their proximity to the men's managers, coaches and players. They really came to life when talking about the men's side of the club, of which they seemed very protective. There was a conservatism (with a small 'c') in the boardroom that I hadn't expected. I've since come to recognise this both as 'football', and as a stance around men's non-league football, and its loyal, slightly ironic and very traditional following.

While our women played in the FA Women's Championship (also known as the Barclays Women's Championship due to the bank sponsoring the two top women's leagues), our men played in the Pitching In Isthmian League. As a new director, I now started to learn about the men's football league system in this country (for full transparency, I must have had it explained to me about five times before it would properly sink in – I had to *make* myself interested at first). While I had always unwittingly thought of 'football' as Premier League football (having known boys and men who supported Liverpool, Manchester United and various world-famous top English teams), I'd never considered the system that fed into those leagues and all the clubs below them.

It turns out that there are no fewer than three professional leagues below the Premier – previously Divisions 1, 2, 3 and 4, but now, since the Premier League was created in 1992, called the English Football League, consisting of the Championship, League One and League Two. Below these four fully professional leagues – still with me? Confusing, isn't it? – there are lots more leagues in non-league football. There's the National League (top level of non-league), then the National League South and the National League North. Lewes FC's men's team is in the league below the National League South. As you can see from the names, the football becomes more and more regionalised the lower we go, to bring down travel costs and increase attendances. You can also see why it's called 'the football pyramid', with so many more teams competing in the lower echelons and fewer at the top. There are four levels of non-league (of which Lewes are in the third), and then below us are the county leagues, split up even more locally and operating all over the country. So there are a multitude of grassroots men's teams in this pyramid, and most of them I'd never heard of at all.

But as I attended men's matches, home and away, and talked to fans, I began to understand that there was a romance to non-league football that was miles away from the newspaper reports and TV games I'd seen. Someone described the fans to me as 'having a preference for authenticity over glamour'. Watching non-league was about loyalty to your team, about taking pride in where you belonged and experiencing your place in a tribe. A tribe that enjoyed warm beer after long train journeys, and would stand in the pouring rain to be the 'twelfth man' any day of the week. I recognised the type in Charlie, a loyal supporter, and incomprehensibly passionate about the team. It was a soul thing, and 'You don't know what you're doing, ref!', 'Up the Lewes!' and 'Come on, you Rooooks!' were the pithy, heartfelt *cris de coeur* shouted into the darkness of sloping, drenched pitches on a midweek evening, all the while anticipating pie, mash and gravy at half-time, maybe followed by a Mars Bar. Sometimes the away matches meant exploring pretty towns or quirky pubs, but often they were home grounds with basic facilities and not much to look at but still plenty to get excited about in terms of the game itself. There was never oat milk for my tea in the directors' hospitality room at these matches. I never – not once – met another female director during half-time. And all the talk was about players, coaches, grounds and league table predictions within non-league football. It was their world. On the plus side, there was absolutely *never* a queue for the ladies' loos.

It felt at first like I was a bit of a threat, or at least an unknown quantity, to some of the board: would I, with my self-proclaimed dislike of men's football and apparently strong passion for the women's game, somehow harm the men's non-league scene? Did I *deserve* my place there in everybody's eyes? My immediate instinct was simply to be nice, and kind of humble, in an effort to gain acceptance and/or respect. I suppose I was an invader of sorts, but I was not an enemy. Quite the opposite. And I also did that thing that so many women do when they feel they don't measure up in men's eyes because their gender works against them. I worked very hard, hardly had a day off, and resented it a bit, despite liking what I was doing.

Sometimes it was difficult to maintain niceness when issues were at stake. I had come to football via gender equality and not the other way around. It seemed clear to me that if we were on a mission – as was now stated on the club's website – to 'set an example on the largest achievable stage', and to 'use football as a vehicle for social change', then shouldn't campaigning and activations be of major importance to the whole board? These things rarely seemed to be talked about unless Ed gave one of his (excellent) visionary speeches, or Charlie introduced an idea and ruffled feathers as 'Lewes FC' on social media. I was a bit baffled, but curious and willing to learn how this football club board operated, never having been on a board before. And I did feel more and more like Alice falling down the rabbit hole, the 'nice' habits of a lifetime falling away the further I dropped.

Running a football club was hard and dedicated graft. I was awed by the amount of work most directors put into the club while holding down day jobs. In many ways they were all exceptional people whom I grew to admire, though not always to agree with. But some of them seemed to find even looking at me during a face-to-face discussion quite difficult.

After my kettle realisation, there was more drama to come at the very next board meeting. At the time, there was an opinion around among a minority of fans that equality was about elevating women *at the expense* of men, when I had a very different understanding of the term. It was raised that I'd arranged for Charlie and me to host three sessions at a local journalism festival on the same day as a men's away match. I'd set up a panel on women's sports in the media, was running a women's football chanting workshop, and would bring along some of our female footballers to put on a 'Skills Session' for newbies to the game. It was thought that my promoting of Lewes FC's participation in the festival might distract attention, and possibly fans, from the match. I was pretty sure it wouldn't, and that the people who wanted to go to the men's away match would travel anyway and not come to the festival, and vice versa. I wondered how much Big Fred (made-up name) – a notional Lewes FC Men's fan who loved to swear at the ref – would appreciate listening to the likes of John Cleese, Lemn Sissay and Pussy Riot, who were due to appear at the festival; perhaps he'd stand up and shout, 'You don't know what you're doing!' from the audience? (At this point in the club's history, the men's and women's teams seemed to operate in silos, so I didn't expect there to be a potential problem for fans. This changed during my time on the board, and the club became more united as management and direction shifted.)

However, I remember a heated discussion about the nature of 'equality' – one of many during my time on the board – where we dissected what the word meant in practical terms within the context of football. Were we promoting the women's team at the men's team's expense? What happened when one team was promoted to a different league? Or relegated? I enjoyed these occasional debates, although they could be stressful because of our strong stances.

It must be asked though – how many football clubs across the country were having passionate discussions about equality around boardroom tables back then? In fact, how many are having them even now? Yes, sometimes we disagreed, bringing our different experiences to the table, but I was glad to offer my perspective. It was refreshing after the inevitable bubbles and echo chambers of my feminist, not-into-football social media crowd!

However, one director sadly resigned just a couple of months after I joined the board and took to social media to publicly announce it. I immediately received a call from BBC Radio Sussex, forewarning me before my regular slot that they had read the director's blog online and would be asking me about it.

He wrote, 'the club has become overwhelmed by the single issue of the equality campaign', continuing, 'I joined a football club and feel like I'm leaving a political party.'

Now, *I* didn't feel equality was party political, but it certainly needed a lot of support behind it if we were to make it work in football, and garnering that support felt fair, justified and the right thing to do. Our football club was at the vanguard of gender equality in sports, and we were bound to attract criticism while struggling to find our way. This 'football-plus-gender-equality-to-serve-a-wider-purpose-in-society' approach hadn't been done before. Happily, most other board members felt as I did, and those who didn't were certainly not concerned, or at least not enough, to literally or metaphorically leave the room.

Meanwhile the festival was fun and earned us some new owners and women's football generally a good amount of interest.

I'd like to make a point here about gender equality in football, and how it was navigated. Sometimes it was a struggle on the board of Lewes FC to find the space to talk about campaigning and activations around women's matches, or the impact work I was excited by and leading on. This was partly because most of the work of the board back then involved the day-to-day, year-on-year *operational* management of the club. But it was also *partly* because the impact work wasn't universally felt to be a priority. I could see that the two areas – impact and operations – fed each other and were, in fact, two sides of the same coin. That is to say, the profile the club was building via its impact served to strengthen its brand, in turn bringing in the money that funded the club's operations and actual playing budgets. Likewise, the higher the quality of the football being played and the better the facilities available, the bigger the platform Lewes FC had from which to make an impact. But for many on the board, the main motivation was the football, and the practical operation of staging matches, more specifically, men's non-league football matches. Making an impact via gender equality and supporting the women's team really wasn't the biggest deal for all of us.

This issue was partly eased for me because the situation clearly reflected society, where the fight for gender equality is not at the forefront of most people's minds. The men on the board appeared to represent the type of men I wanted to engage with about gender equality – those who might not prioritise it naturally but are open to supporting when prompted to consider it. I suspect this describes many men. So the board was a good practice area! Engaging in these conversations was valuable learning, as was trying to understand the perspectives of some male football fans on the board. It was helpful to remember the unattributed quote flying around in diversity and inclusion circles: 'For somebody who is accustomed to privilege, equality feels like oppression.' I kept this in mind, recognising that my presence on the board – as a woman, someone without a prior interest in football and someone guided by feminist principles – might make some people feel uncomfortable or unsettled. And I tried to keep my touch light, but, you know, firm.

Prior to Equality FC, Lewes FC Men was a typical non-league team, consisting of relatively local Sussex or south London lads. (To most of their fans, they were of course known as 'Lewes FC'; it had only been the women's team who were initially distinguished by their gender, as 'Lewes Ladies'.) Managers were sourced from a familiar pool where everyone seemed to know each other – I'd heard it referred to as 'the Sussex merry-go-round'. Slowly I grew to see a correlation between the women's game in general at this stage of its development (2019) and the men's non-league game. Both struggled financially: players were part-time footballers who often had other full-time jobs, because most of the money in football was concentrated in the higher leagues. Both the Isthmian League and the Women's Championship were at once romantic and unglamorous – clusters of loyal fans supporting their teams no matter what the weather, the shoddy location, the result. And much to my amusement, many fans on both touchlines seemed under the impression that they themselves were the manager, shouting at players and giving their tuppence-worth afterwards to anyone who'd listen.

The intimacy and accessibility afforded by pitchside selfies and autographs also united the two games. It did seem fair back then to pay and resource both these teams the same, even though, of course, the women were playing at a much higher level than the men. Our scenario underlined the fact that because women and girls had been under-resourced and underdeveloped in football for so long, there was currently an equivalency to be drawn between Lewes FC Women and Lewes FC Men. As the women's game developed, it might be that this equivalency would be tested, and we would need to talk more about *equity* than equality at Lewes. However, for now, we were on a journey together, and some on the board were further along the path of women's empowerment in football than others, depending on where passions and interests lay. If the club continued to grow according to its mission to create social change, I was confident that the board's composition would alter over the next few years, and that we would see more advocates of change in both the boardroom and the club's office, as indeed we already were among our ever-growing ownership.

Meanwhile, I launched many reports on our campaigning work and relationship-building. But they seemed to drift into a void of board tumbleweed. The silence was sometimes deafening. The lack of response to the campaigning, engagement and impact work was hard to take at times, both as a newbie and given my distinctly felt lack of footballing authority on the board, but then I was also aware that other board members felt similarly about their own interest areas. In an effort to change karma (i.e., stop fantasising about how underqualified, inappropriate or weird I was, and start thinking about other people), I did what every good Buddhist does and tried to show appreciation for all the stuff that didn't immediately grab *my* interest, while also making use of the gratitude journal Ed had thoughtfully given me to record things I was grateful for about the club and other board members. It could be that someone had included me in a conversation; or that they *hadn't*, and so I'd had the chance to 'woman' up, butt in and include myself. I have an entry that reads, 'Grateful for ★★★★ not bothering to turn up to the board meeting today – we were able to get through the whole agenda', and, more winningly, '★★★★ gave me a smile as I came in'. The smallest things were worth writing down and noting, and thanking colleagues personally was another step forward, until gratitude became a bit of a habit. It wasn't easy; it was definitely a bit corny at first, but it was better than shrinking in this Wonderland and crying like Alice because I wasn't sure of my place here. Like the footballers who inspired me on the pitch, here on the board I was learning resilience, and *that* was certainly something to be grateful for.

Chapter 14
Deeds *And* Words

———

How can we effect change in the world when only
half of it is invited?

Emma Watson

According to Carl Rogers – the father of person-centred counselling – we all have a 'locus of evaluation'. While it's tempting to think of this as a *locust*, a kind of insect daemon, perching on our shoulder in the manner of Jiminy Cricket as Pinocchio's conscience, it does in fact refer to the way in which we evaluate ourselves. As in, what am I worth? In my counselling career, I got to know not only my own locus, but a lot of other people's too, and let me tell you, those things can move around. It was my job as a counsellor to help people gradually relocate their locus from external towards internal. This movement would forge a path to encourage you to stop judging yourself by what other people thought of you and develop your own inner standards instead, so bringing you closer to what Rogers called your 'organismic self' (real self, if you like).

Rogers believed that we're all affected by 'conditions of worth' from the get-go, and that these are reinforced by social rules and conventions: we get praise when we do acceptable things, and negative feedback when we don't. One of the most important therapeutic goals of a good counselling relationship is to provide an environment where there are no conditions of worth, and the client feels valued unconditionally. For a counsellor, this means establishing empathy, being as transparent as is helpful with your feelings, and having 'unconditional positive regard' for the client, no matter their behaviours. For example, if one of my own conditions of worth was 'I've got to get to therapy bang on time or else my therapist will hold a grudge against me', I would find that the therapist still valued me, and held the space and time for me, regardless of my lateness (they might explore the lateness with me, of course, but they still rated me as a human!). If one of my client's conditions of worth was 'I'm not a real man unless I play or follow football' (just keeping on subject here), then I might challenge that idea with him and hopefully do the relationship work to establish that he was a whole and wonderful man whether or not he decided to give football the time of day.

So how does this relate to being an outsider in an organisation? As both a former client and a former therapist, I can attest that it's a great thing for your value in this world to be free of anyone else's opinions, so that you judge yourself by your own standards, via a sound therapeutic relationship. But being on the board of

Modelling card

KAREN

The Rooks 125 – Alex Leith,
Patrick Marber, Nick Williams,
Ben Ward, Ed Ramsden and
Charlie Dobres – plotting in
the Brewers Arms

Equality FC publicity photograph, July 2017

Karen and the Suffragette Flashmob, February 2018

Karen Dobres, Charlie Dobres, Jackie Gilligan, Glenda
Thomas, John Donoghue and Ed Ramsden at Wembley
for the Championship interview, April 2018

Karen talking at a Kickass Women event

Jess King, Sammy Quayle, Katie McIntyre and Emma Jones get that scoring feeling at the Pan, 2019

James Boyes

The Beach Huts in use

Pitch side sign under the TV gantry

Marios Christos Sfantos, Lucy Mills, Karen Dobres and Kelly Lindsey
at the Athens Women's Football Summit, September 2022

Karen and Stef for Veo (Lewes FC sponsors)
campaign 'Play For More'

The state-of-the-art pitch at The Dripping Pan

'Inexorable' by Amanda Cotton
– rejected by a Devon council,
welcomed by Lewes FC –
standing tall

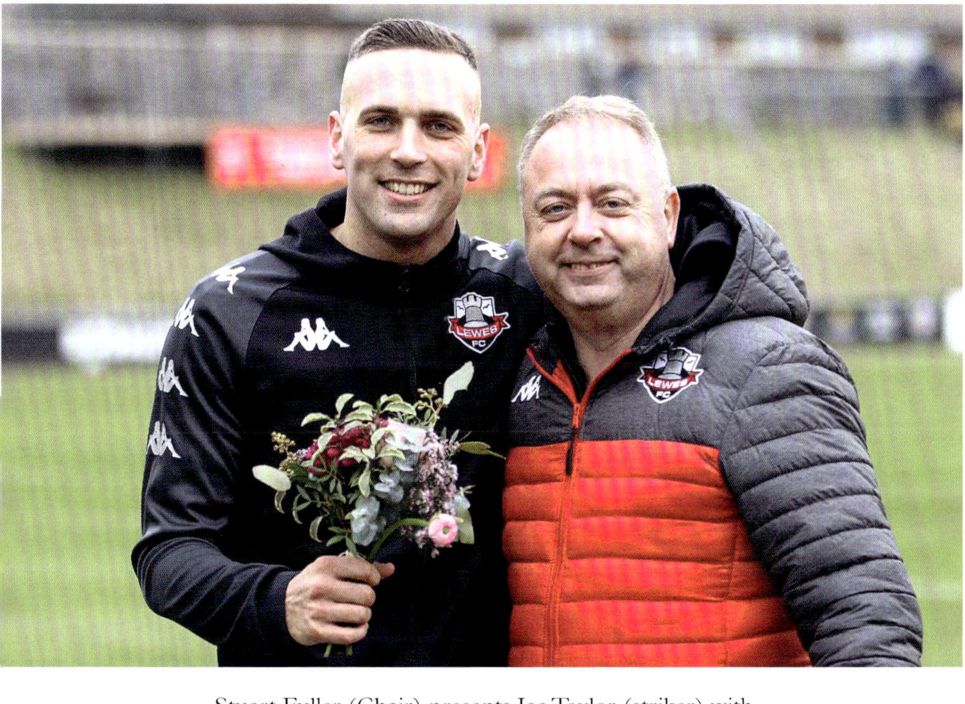

Stuart Fuller (Chair) presents Joe Taylor (striker) with
a handtied bouquet for Player of the Match

Volunteers (including Bradley Pritchard) get 'radishal' at Brad's Pit

Matchday poster featuring women's captain, Rhian Cleverly

a football club was a bit like the opposite of sitting in any kind of therapy room, and sometimes proved a massive challenge to *my* good old locus! Never mind unconditional positive regard; it was sometimes unusual to find *any* regard at all! I'm laughing as I write because I'm thinking of women in STEM, politics and film, who have shared similar experiences of being almost *dramatically* overlooked. They would barely be greeted, if at all, they'd be interrupted and spoken over, no one would make eye contact with them . . . I was learning, after my contrasting experiences in the worlds of fashion and therapy, that in football, interpersonal skills and relationship-building were not everyone's strong point.

Given this frequent lack of regard, it was useful to win awards for the club's off-pitch achievements because they validated my work championing gender equality. It's an uphill struggle to stay determined to change things when you're getting little feedback, and therapy isn't always an inside job, let's face it. So here's to a bit of external validation, the joy it brings, and the news that in 2019, Lewes FC became a finalist in UN Women UK's HeForShe Awards.

Have you heard of UN Women UK? I confess that up until 2019, I didn't know much about them. I knew of the UN's Sustainable Development Goals from Buddhist writings about how to achieve world peace, but hadn't studied them, and couldn't have told you back then that 'Achieve gender equality and empower all women and girls by 2030' was goal no. 5. But on hearing the news that we were finalists, Ed and Charlie were buzzing. So was our chair, Stu Fuller. It would be both unusual (unique at this point in time) and prestigious for a football club to win an award from a distinguished organisation campaigning for women's rights. And pioneers that we were, being shortlisted validated the Equality FC decision, giving a strong signal that, as disruptors, we were on the right path. We didn't know who had nominated us, but we were glad that the bold decision to raise the women's playing budget to match the men's had been recognised for its audacity and its singularity. And, frankly, the minority of grumblers about Equality FC could stick that in their whistles and blow it.

I researched HeForShe and watched a video of the actor Emma Watson at the launch of the campaign in 2014 as she implored men to act on behalf of women in order to change gender inequality across the world. Defining the essential belief of feminism as men and women getting equal resources and opportunities, she reclaimed the word 'feminism' itself from a growing backlash against it. The speech was inspiring and made a lot of sense. I could see why HeForShe was interested in a football club – the theme was *'engaging men'*.

It was decided that myself, Stu and Ed would meet at the central London venue and answer the interview panel's questions. It was a fancy corporate place and Ed and Stu wore suits. (This was remarkable in itself, what with Ed's favourite joke being that we were 'the scruffiest football club board ever'. To which I'd always reply, with a side-eye to his trackie bottoms and sliders, 'Speak for yourself.') We were met by a friendly young man called Simon, who accompanied us up several floors in a lift, showed us to a waiting area and then made chit-chat about football as he pointed out the sights through the huge windows overlooking the City of London. I noticed that while I was having a great back-and-forth with Simon – thankfully avoiding the nuances of the history of men's football – the men seemed quieter than usual. This surprised me – both Ed and Stu spoke plenty at board meetings – until I realised that, for once, it wasn't me who was feeling like the odd one out. I was actually looking forward to this interview. Feminism is one of my favourite subjects and an area in which I feel pretty knowledgeable. But the guys seemed unusually on edge. Could it be that Lewes FC's fish out of water had, for once, landed in a pond she recognised?

We were directed to a corridor where a group of dreadlocked black women emerged from a room, dressed to the nines and confident. They'd just been interviewed. Relaxed and smiling, I exchanged a friendly 'hi', and then it was our turn. The three of us sat facing a desk of six judges, mainly women, and answered a variety of questions. Stu and Ed were confident and articulate, but I felt they'd missed the point of one of the questions. The judges seemed to be looking for an answer that would highlight to them any discussions we were having with men who wouldn't normally be discussing equal pay and resources for female footballers. This was my cue to tell them about the Equality FC campaign and the way we'd introduced it to our mostly male fan base ('How do you tell your daughter she's worth less than your son?'). I was honest in explaining that not everyone had reacted well to it, that there had been objections. But I emphasised how exciting the response had been from sponsors and new owners, and in the turnout at women's games. 'People are voting for equal pay in football with their money and their attendance,' I explained, 'and it's inspiring to witness. Some men are coming back to football, to our *women's* matches, because they've been turned off the toxic masculinity tolerated by aspects of the men's game. It's gratifying, and bodes well for gender equality off the pitch. We hope to influence other clubs.'

We left the room unsure about how we'd gone down, but knowing we'd done our best. Some weeks later, I got an email from Simon inviting me along with 'all the finalists' to the awards ceremony for the 'equality trailblazers'. The board agreed that we probably hadn't won since they were inviting just one person, but that we'd done well to get shortlisted. I dressed up and went along to the event in Mayfair, greeted by a glass of champagne and lots of glamorous people. After the reception – in which comedian, author and host of the *Guilty Feminist* podcast, Deborah Frances-White, gave a moving speech about practical inclusion and making an effort to talk to people we didn't know, including each other right there and then (music to my ears, arriving solo and not knowing anyone; I decided this amounted to full permission to be my usual self despite the number of dignitaries probably present) – we were ushered to yet another big room full of lavishly laid tables.

As a side note, inclusion as an action is extremely important to me. To feel included and to include others into your circle can make a whole day go well. I realise that my mother – as one of eleven children in a big Anglo-Irish family – has taught me lessons about it all my life without me knowing it. In fact, the idea of 'networking' is very familiar to me: it's basically what she used to do when we travelled around on buses in the school holidays, various young cousins and neighbours' children along for the ride with us. Except we didn't call it networking then, it was our normal. By the end of any journey, we'd be on first-name terms with everyone on the bus, and according to Mum, they were all 'our friends'! I always thought that Mum pulling some grass out of a dog's throat to save a woman going to the vet (dog cured, the surprised woman disembarked at the next stop and went gratefully home), or offering to cut another passenger's hair the next day in our front room (they did have to wear a hat for weeks afterwards, but it was the thought that counted) was perfectly unremarkable behaviour.

So as usual, this afternoon in Mayfair, I was ready to make new friends on this plush 'bus' and see who could help whom. I found myself seated next to some inspiring finalists. I chatted to a female entrepreneur – Sharmadean Reid – who was creating communities for women, sharing her hard-earned lessons in business. And I met Elliott Rae, who had founded MusicFootballFatherhood, creating space for like-minded men and advocating to give men equal caring rights as well as pushing for the social change needed to do that. I felt at home with these people, but was not prepared for the moment when a video of me on local Brighton TV talking about the important role football could have in achieving gender equality appeared, on a giant screen, and it was announced that Lewes FC had won the HeForShe 'inspiration' award!

I got up and stumbled through an impromptu speech in front of all the honourable guests as I accepted the award on behalf of the club and our owners around the world. As soon as I was sitting down again, I messaged the directors' online messaging channel, pinging them a picture of our award with shaky hands. Everyone was ecstatic. I thought I could feel the air being punched in their various locations as they sent messages asking for more pictures to put on our socials. No one had expected this win, and we were all gobsmacked. It was extremely validating for our hard-working board, and, I admit, for me personally, having been out there pressing the issue.

Afterwards, I chatted to the CEO of UN Women UK ('Get me!'), who explained how impressed the judges were at 'the stand Lewes has taken', and that 'the top earner among your players is a woman'. This was true, because although our managers got equal budgets, it was entirely up to them how they divvied out the money among players. It was another great statistic to quote that underlined our difference in the male-dominated football space. But I told the CEO that as we spoke, there were Lionesses out there who couldn't afford to go out for a cappuccino ('And that is from the mouth of a former Lioness,' I added, because it was). Women footballers were valued nothing like male ones, and it was shameful, and yet we were the only club with the credibility to draw attention to this fact. She told me the judges had also been impressed that in the last season our home attendances had been second only to Manchester United in our division. I was delighted that we'd been noticed and applauded. And we wouldn't be stopping here, I thought, getting the Tube back to Victoria station, handbag full of business cards again and buoyed up by all the great people trying to change the world right where they were.

Around about this time, my good friend Fiona invited me for lunch in London. We went to her favourite restaurant, *Caldesi in Marylebone*. I'd not been before, but Fiona explained that she'd often popped in with her late mum and the place held some special memories. As we chatted away, I told her about the award from UN Women UK, and she was suitably impressed. Like so many of my friends, Fiona had never given football a second glance but was now an owner at Lewes FC, after attending a talk by Katie Rood and myself at a pub in south London. We'd been invited by the Southwark branch of the Women's Equality Party to talk on the theme 'How to Grab Equal Pay by the Balls'. We scored lots of ownerships that night! Fiona was yet to come to a match, though.

As we chatted, we became more and more aware of a couple directly to our left evidently having trouble with a wonky table. The man was asking very loudly for something to wedge under one of the legs so that the tabletop would be level, and the smartly dressed woman was very animated and speaking loudly too. Both were freely switching between Italian and English and seemingly in very good, if remarkably demanding, spirits. They were hard to ignore. Typical understated Brits, Fiona and I smiled very briefly in their direction to acknowledge their predicament, as waiters rushed around attentively, trying their best to rectify the situation. The man, in his sixties – smart, smiling, charismatic – leaned over to us to ask how we were enjoying our lunch. And so began a jovial conversation with . . . Mr Caldesi himself, and his dining partner, front-of-house manager Georgia.

Fiona had met restaurateur, author and TV chef Giancarlo Caldesi before, as he often greets guests warmly and chats to them, and he seemed to recognise her. She introduced me, telling him I was a football club director and that the club had just won an award for gender equality.

Giancarlo regarded me with surprise and interest. 'You? You are a football club director? Which club? How is this?' he asked, genuinely curious.

I explained briefly, and his eyes nearly popped out of his head. 'But women are not made to play football!' he exclaimed. Georgia smiled warmly at us, rolling her eyes, saying that equal pay in football was the best idea *she'd* heard in some time.

It has to be said that Mr Caldesi was, in his charming way, initially quite disparaging about the idea of Equality FC, and not convinced that women should be playing football at all, never mind getting the same wages as men for doing so. During our conversation that afternoon, which was to take many twists and turns and feature many imagined scenarios in which women might not be as strong or as capable as men, Giancarlo shared that among his unusual professional occupations in the past – from paratrooper to celebrity chef – he had once played for Romford FC. He was a great fan of the men's game, but flanked by Georgia, who was already swept up with the romance of equal pay in football; Fiona, who, though she wasn't a football fan, was incredibly proud of what we achieved in Lewes; and myself, an unlikely football club director banging on about our amazing female players who stood to change the world, well, he was outnumbered. His generosity of spirit led him to rethink his position. Our conversation that lunchtime – which most definitely involved using our outdoor voices indoors – covered a lot of ground. Who would survive longer in a desert without food, man or woman? What is the best method for making roast potatoes? How might the speed at which female players run affect (or not) one's cumulative enjoyment of a match?

What had been a quiet and private catch-up between Fiona and me developed into more of a party, with Mr Caldesi ordering champagne, gifting us cookery books and vowing to come to the Dripping Pan to watch a match with me. I'm pleased to say we're still good friends.

True to his word, he joined me and one of my friends from BBC Radio Sussex, presenter Amanny Mo, at Lewes v London Bees in 2019, bringing his son Giorgio along for the ride. It was a lot of fun, not least because Giorgio and Amanny introduced themselves to fans together ('We're Giorgio Armani'), bringing a touch of high fashion to the Pan. Our gregarious Italian won over everyone he met that day with humour, passion and friendliness. In turn, spirited play from our women's team won *him* over and he became a big fan of Lewes FC and the equality initiative. A couple of months later, he invited me to bring the whole team up to London to his restaurant, where we were treated like queens, enjoying a delicious three-course meal ('like Nonna used to make') and drinks. The players were delighted, if somewhat bemused, by all the attention, and we had a wonderful time.

As we were in London, a group of us popped into the National Portrait Gallery after lunch. I'd noted that an exhibition called 'Pre-Raphaelite Sisters' was on – billed as exploring 'the overlooked contribution of twelve women to this iconic artistic movement' – and had written to the gallery to ask for complimentary tickets for our women, who had similarly been routinely overlooked by society. They kindly put some free tickets on the door, saying they were keen to diversify their audience. Indeed, most of our group hadn't been to a major art exhibition before, and for a couple of players, it was only their first or second time in London. These were dedicated young footballers, and though they had played around the world, spare time for cultural outings was minimal. It was a real pleasure to walk round the gallery with them, taking in the art, thinking about how women had been ignored, diminished and marginalised in so many arenas, believing we were changing that.

Reaching the end of the exhibition, I spotted the animated group sitting around the life-sized pop-up heads of the pre-Raphaelite brothers who had got all the fame (Rossetti, Waterhouse, Collinson, Stephens, et al.), laughing and jostling as if they were in a changing room.

'What's going on?' I asked Roodie.

'We're doing snog, marry, avoid with them,' said our star striker. 'Only it's regressed to snog, marry, kill!'

Yeah, that was our girls. Creative, fun and taking no shit from anyone who'd try and make them into a muse.

Having met the team, and in the name of equality, Mr Caldesi decided to sponsor a Lewes double-header,[15] bringing his wife, Katie, to stay over in the town for the weekend. He shared a recipe for the players' post-match meal (a tasty pasta dish with bacon and onions), co-commentated on the matches from our TV gantry and, in a typically generous gesture, brought his chosen players of the match and their partners to dinner at his Marylebone restaurant. His commentary was fantastic, prompting American owners listening in on the live stream to comment: 'Who is this mad Italian predicting Ollie Tanner[16] to be the next Pele? Genius addition to the match!!'

Un caro salute, Giancarlo.

And now, an advertising break.

Charlie had taken on the design of the matchday posters a few years after the club became fan-owned. His advertising agency background coming to the fore, he'd gone out of his way to make these posters work on multiple levels. At first, he designed posters just for the men's team. After all, the women's team didn't officially amalgamate into the club until the 2013–14 season.

---

15 A double-header is when there are two games over the same weekend at the same venue – one for the men's team and one for the women's.

16 Ollie Tanner is a young winger who, at the time of going to print, plays professional football for Cardiff City FC in the men's Championship. He transferred there after a highly successful season at Lewes in 2021– 22, where he scored 13 goals in 34 appearances.

And, influenced by the community ownership, he pointedly associated the posters with popular culture, drawing football into an engaging mix of literature, music and film, and referencing phenomena ranging from the well known to the – it has to be said – slightly obscure. I once asked him why some of the references were so bloody hard to work out – 'Who has even *heard* of that album?' I'd ask, befuddled by a poster I'd seen somewhere in town. He explained that people would see the poster opposite the station, or in a shop window, and wonder about it, even talk about it. Eventually they'd get the reference – maybe not first time, but after repeated exposure, or they might go as far as asking someone about it, so spreading the interest. And in getting it, they'd become part of a community, an 'in-group' if you like, who understood and were sharing a knowing laugh.

The posters were witty and worked hard – people uninterested in football admired them. Eye-catching in themselves, they felt cool and captivating. And sometimes that was all I got from them, unless I asked! An example? OK. Picture a single yellow French fry, diagonally placed across a white background, with the title 'The Lewes Football Club and Chipstead'. What could this be about? Why was there a chip on a poster by Lewes station? Because of Chipstead? Well, not *just* that, dear Reader! Oh no. This was – of course (not) – a reference to *The Velvet Underground & Nico*, the debut studio album by the American rock band and a German singer. According to Wikipedia, this particular album 'underperformed in sales and polarized critics upon release due to its abrasive, unconventional sound and controversial lyrical content'. The album cover features a Warhol print of a banana lying across a white background in the same way as our French fry. The font is exactly the same. No way would I, in a million years, have got this reference. But when I really understood one of these posters (one of the ones that even, as Charlie liked to say, 'a total thickie' could get), I felt slightly proud of myself – I was part of the cool gang, I knew the score.

'The Rook in the Book', anyone?

'Rookz' washing powder?

Maybe Obama's 'Hope' image with the slightly manic-looking cartoon rook designed by our friend Dave Shephard?

I loved Charlie's Banksy-inspired poster of two kissing policemen when Lewes FC Men played the Met Police. The posters were picked up by the press, who claimed variously that they'd achieved 'a cult following', were 'a splendid array of witty posters' and 'some of the finest matchday posters we've ever seen', and that 'non-league Lewes FC have cornered the market in witty matchday posters'.

So what would Charlie do for the women's team?

Well, he worked to his own ongoing brief to place football among the other main cultural movements in the country (art, politics, music, etc.) but to do it *tonally*, i.e., in a way that was on brand (read quirky, funny, irreverent, self-deprecating). When Equality FC was first introduced as the name of our movement and marketing campaign, posters advertised men's and women's match dates *together*, and depicted famous couples. We saw Annie Lennox and Dave Stewart, Sid and Nancy, Antony and Cleopatra,

Bonnie and Clyde, John and Yoko – famous duos known for a fairly equal distribution of power in their relationships.

The second season (2018–19) saw inspirational women from the away team's locale fronting the women's matchday posters, stylishly drawn by local pop artist Chris Arran, working to Charlie's brief, and featuring a detail of one of our players alongside the larger face of a famous woman. We were honouring our opponents by referencing one of their local greats (comedian Kathy Burke for Arsenal, musician Joan Armatrading for Aston Villa, actor/campaigner Vanessa Redgrave for Charlton, Helen Sharman, the first British astronaut, for Sheffield United, etc.), drawing attention to the solidarity and sisterhood that exists in the women's game. Women's football was a small world, and players supported each other in the struggle to be validated and resourced enough to play, so we would recognise and respect the away team, and correct the underrepresentation of high-achieving women, while of course being *competitive as hell* on the pitch! It didn't hurt the club's profile, of course, when Joan Armatrading or Kathy Burke retweeted their posters to their followers or commented on the post when tagged.

This kind of targeted marketing campaign with strategic aims, a strong brief and strong artwork was unheard of in women's football at this point. No one, it seemed, was thinking about women's games in these terms or had acted in a way that gave them the credibility to market to women like this. When you're paying and resourcing women properly to play football, 'letting' them compete on the same pitch as your men, giving them private medical treatment when they're injured and working to develop their post-footballing careers too, you've earned the right to shout about your women's team to new markets! The truth was, many clubs, at this point, barely produced posters to tell people the time and location of their women's matches. Numerous matches in the Championship (yes, the second-highest tier) were still attended mainly by friends and families of the players and a few stalwart fans.

For some time, as news of Equality FC and 'little Lewes' – the only club in the world to treat women fairly – spread far and wide, we had been picking up owners in far-flung parts of the world. It was wonderful to know that there were people who might never visit the Pan but nevertheless wanted to express their support in this tangible way, signing up and paying their £50 from the other side of the planet. Gender inequality is a worldwide habit, and though we might not have it as bad as some countries, and we might not have been a rich and powerful football club (yet!), we were evidence that there were people in a little corner of England changing this normalised but harmful thinking, and that as a result of this investment, we might have more of an impact on the world. In Ed's words, we were 'sending out little beams of hope across the world'. I wrote that simple but true quote from Ed as a note to self – a constant reminder on my office wall of what we were trying to do and why.

In season 2018–19, with Equality FC well established, and us becoming more aware of our wider impact, Charlie was inspired to 'go global' with the matchday posters. This time inspirational women from different countries graced the artwork, reimagined in footballing positions.

Perhaps my favourite was Sweden's climate change campaigner Greta Thunberg, who had warned us all that 'our house is burning'. Greta was turned into a goalkeeper for the Lewes v Blackburn Rovers poster, saving the world, which was in turn reimagined as a football. I also loved Lewes v Sheffield, featuring Manal al-Sharif, the Saudi Arabian woman who had successfully campaigned for the driving ban on women in her country to be repealed. She leaned casually against Lewes FC's minibus, a smile playing around her lips, in her imaginary role as our women's team's minibus driver. And then there was South Africa's Phumzile Mlambo-Ngcuka – the then director of UN Women worldwide – as a referee holding up the red card to gender inequality.

The list of great women went on as more matches were played, and it was a joy to showcase the posters – works of art in their own right, but with so much purpose behind them – to the women I would go and talk to about gender equality in football. They were beautiful and inspiring, they explained the subtle but important details of our fledgling movement, they were artistic engineering. More than any of this, though, they were something else in my environment that told me it was OK to be referencing stuff *outside* of football from *within* it. These posters were the bridge between women who didn't like football and football itself – they provided a way across the gaping divide, they were appealing signposts to my unwelcome women that it was all right to take the road less travelled. And they still decorate my office walls today. I don't mean to big up Charlie – God forbid! – but, you know, the sometime 'poster boy' done good.

As we moved forward into the 2020 pandemic, and football stopped, and then restarted behind closed doors, I had a meeting with a young design duo called Sisterhood, a social enterprise working with young girls (aged 13–17) to build confidence through social action projects. They were congratulatory about our equality work and wondered if they might join the growing SisterShips network. The co-founders, Rebecca and Rachita, had recently made a video for Hackney Laces[17] and were looking to continue their creative work within football with girls. It struck me that they might upskill our pathway girls (these were the girls playing in Lewes FC's under-14s and under-16s teams) in graphic design, over Zoom due to the Lockdown, and get them to make our matchday posters for the women's team that season. Sisterhood loved the idea, as did our pathways coordinator, Alison Palmer – a keen photographer herself – and so a project was born. The girls would interview and photograph their heroes from the first team over Zoom, and then use the picture and their favourite pull quotes to make the posters.

So Sisterhood joined our SisterShips, and 15 girls from our pathways learned photography skills, interview and presentation techniques, design tips, Photoshop, and how to receive feedback. They spoke with their first-team role models and had a series of regular online educational sessions with Sisterhood. Feedback was fantastic from parents and carers, and Alison said she could

17 Hackney Laces is a community-based football club in East London, which focuses on empowering girls and women through football.

see the confidence they'd gained in the poster project translating to confidence on the pitch. All Sisterhood's projects were 100 per cent girl-led, with the intention of empowering girls to be leaders and change-makers in their own lives and communities, fitting perfectly with our 100 per cent community-owned football club's mission to use football as a vehicle for social change.

For me, it was a poignant project. The slightly blurry Zoom photos of our players appearing all over town, with encouraging quotes from those players, noted down by young girls and turned into posters, were beautiful and accurate reflections of this strange time we were all living through. The posters were cultural markers. I loved watching masked schoolkids walk past the large one by the station and take a look. The posters represented two of the qualities I had already learned at Lewes FC – teamwork and resilience – and made me feel, yet again, proud of our football club and privileged to be a director.

Chapter 15
Embracing the Imposter

———

Let's reframe what it means to feel imposter syndrome.

Steven Bartlett

Sometimes it's a physical feeling. It shoots upwards from your feet, making you a bit unsteady. Then the sensation seeps through limbs and torso, the blood rising to your face and you might feel a kind of fear. Also, you now look weird and unrelaxed. You're self-conscious as hell. Your nerves wake up, standing on end, uncomfortable, alert to threat. You feel tight, stressed, caught in a glare; your face and palms may be cold with sweat. Have you been found out? You wish you were smaller, that you could retreat to somewhere more hospitable. This is clearly not the right place for you. The language, the customs, the environment – everything pushes you away, it doesn't speak to you, and worse, everyone else is part of the gang. Maybe they *mean* to exclude you? Maybe they see you're different? Are you a freak in their eyes? Are you perhaps a freak, like, full stop?

Sound familiar? For me it is. Many years of my life have been dominated by the sense of being an outsider. I'm used to feeling slightly on the outside of things, and as if people aren't sure which lens to view me through. It's remarkable, when I mention this feeling to others, how *very many* people relate. This could be why it's more comfortable to stay in our own bubble, our opinions reinforced, our tribe nurturing our often fragile self-belief, familiar interactions comforting us – but as my nana might have said, will that get any parsnips buttered in the great big wide, unequal world?

I've learned to navigate my weirdness by being as accommodating as possible (remember the kettle?), by being friendly while in the throes of stressful feelings (men's football terraces) and by trying to find out what I have in common with people, rather than focusing too much on what makes us different (business meetings). I've acquired the handy life skill of moving through potentially awkward or unusual situations with performative ease. While modelling, I had to get to know a new group of people pretty quickly every time I did a job, or win over a new set of 'judges' at every casting. As a counsellor, I encountered diverse people with various issues and problems and formed strong relationships with them. In many working situations I've felt at once slightly on the outside, a little cowed, but nevertheless strangely unshockable, remaining interested in and easy-going with people. This disposition became a skill that served me well at first in my role at Lewes FC, in the new-to-me culture of English football.

For my first years in football, I was an innocent abroad. Listening, watching, asking questions, absorbing, and quite enjoying the apparent contrast, noted gleefully by friends, family and strangers alike, between who they thought I was and the fact that I was now a director of a football club.

I well remember getting a black cab to a venue in east London where I was about to speak on a panel. The cab driver and I were chatting about weather, our children, the theatre, the great suspension in his cab, when he filled one of those conversational lulls by asking what *I* did. Never have I been so close to an accident on the road than when I answered, truthfully, 'Oh, I'm a football club director.' The poor man kept turning around to check me out, exclaiming, 'Well I *never* would have guessed!' and 'Yes! Yeeeesssss! I've heard of Lewes,' and turning out to be an aficionado of both men's non-league and Arsenal. He was at once truly surprised and almost joyful! Of course, he then tried to share memories of football games with me, and what had previously been a rollicking back-and-forth conversation became a bit one-sided. Nevertheless, I appreciated that I'd now acquired this extra language, my social reach had expanded, and certain people might feel a bit more at home with me by virtue of the role.

Never mind my gender, I was also a 'football virgin' – a person who had not had the sport in my life before, and so had never learned the culture of team banter, dressing in trackies, or the endless high-fiving and fist-bumping greetings. So strange, so befuddling, yet so endearing. I was far more used to hugging, air-kissing, thinking about a different outfit each day and the endless application of lipstick, I'm afraid. But I was now fully aware – with information coming from both women who didn't like football and men who did – that I was a bit of a conundrum, and that my being involved in football was, well, disruptive. In my fifties by now, I wasn't going to try to change myself or my lipstick habit, but I was certainly not averse to learning about a new culture and how to connect with it.

By December 2018, our women's team had a new manager, Fran Alonso, who had joined us from Spain. Having previously worked with the (apparently) well-known men's manager Mauricio Pochettino, Fran was very keen both on coaching women *and* on Lewes FC's messages of equality, which had spread to Spain. As a young man in Madrid, he had felt 'physically disgusted' when his sister's football team had been asked by male managers to wear short skirts. Caffeinated to the hilt with an endless supply of green maté tea and immediately purchasing Lewes FC ownerships for his entire family back in Spain, he was clearly 'one of us' (i.e., obsessive, on a mission, seeing a bigger picture) and we all had high hopes.

Playing Manchester United away in May 2019 was a big deal for the team, for Fran and for the few of us Rooks who made it to the match. Were we off to the famous, iconic Old Trafford? No, we were not. The game was played at Leigh Sports Village Stadium. Even as I write this now, a few years down the line, Manchester United Women still rarely play at 'the men's stadium'. Honestly, what is wrong with people's minds that they still excuse this kind of biased and short-term decision-making in football clubs?

I think there were about eight of us from Lewes there and most were in the directors' box. We were fully aware that we, frankly one of the poorest clubs in elite football, were being hosted by the richest club in the world. In fact, when a United fan tweeted that we were 'a poverty club' and they'd 'wipe the floor' with us, Lewes FC Women (as in, Charlie) retorted simply, 'Thanks for the team talk.' Got lots of retweets. Anyway, what we lacked in money we made up for in the respect *our* club had for its women's team.

But our team *were* envious when they saw the matching wheelie suitcases that the United players brought to the changing rooms. Bloody hell. I decided to research luggage companies upon my return. Maybe someone would give us red and black wheelies for our team? As usual, I refused to believe that a company wouldn't want to come on that journey of equality with Lewes FC. I also couldn't bear our players to look like the poor relations when to my mind they were the plucky underdog warriors who had fought and sacrificed to be here, using principles, skill and determination. And crucially, they'd achieved it without money from a rich men's team. Our players were symbols of our disruptor brand as much as I was, a non-football person showing up in football.

Following the talk I'd given at Brighton Chamber of Commerce, a very kind and talented milliner called Joanna Zara spontaneously designed a hat for me. After calling me to her studio for a fitting, she gifted me a beautiful felt red fedora with a black ribbon, a rook's feather and a little silver castle. I was absolutely chuffed. It might just be the best present I've ever had!

But a question kept popping into my head – how on earth was I going to wear it on the terraces? I had taken to wearing Lewes football shirts to matches, usually tucked into jeans, with gloves, layers of thermals, a jacket or two and a couple of beanies on my head. Sometimes I topped the look off with some nice boots, and always, *always* a red lip. Would a fedora be a bit much? However, this match, against arguably the most famous club in the world, one that even *I'd* heard of, where we were invited to sit in the hospitality boxes . . . this felt like the right occasion to wear a bespoke hat. So wear it I did.

In the box we were served champagne by uniformed waiters, and a delicious three-course meal, complete with cutlery and crisp, white linen serviettes – the extravagance! The manager of Manchester United's men's team, Ole Gunnar Solskjaer, was seated on one side of us with his family (of course, I'd no idea who he was until someone told me), and the Mayor of Manchester, Andy Burnham (I knew who he was!), on the other. A far cry from our funny, humble beach huts,[18] with pie 'n' mash to one side, and

---

18 Our four beach huts were introduced to the club by Charlie in 2014, initially as an April Fool's Day joke. However, fans deemed them a good idea, so Charlie brought in the six-person huts to serve as executive boxes – but Lewes FC-style. Each little hut sports a kettle, tea bags, coffee and a sign saying 'No prawn sandwiches' (apparently standard hospitality fare at posh football matches). Although they are undoubtedly unusual for a football club – or anywhere not by the seaside, in fact – the Dripping Pan is just eight miles from the English Channel as the rook flies, and I can personally vouch for them as an ideal venue for a birthday party should yours fall on a matchday.

Barbara with the raffle tickets and Gary the Badge[19] to the other. But *our* stadium was characterful, joyful and – significantly – equally home to both the men *and* the women.

Members of Manchester United Women's fan group, the Barmy Army, ably led by irrepressible uber-fan Natalie Burrell, told me they liked my fedora. Since Lewes fans were thin on the ground, I thought nothing of having a quick word in Nat's ear. I gave her the team sheets we'd been provided with in our box, and in exchange, she kindly agreed to lead some chants for our players. I knew this was unusual (whoever heard of fans chanting for an opposing team?), but I also knew that Lewes held a special place in the Man U fans' hearts, because we'd been so welcoming (naturally) to them when they'd visited the Dripping Pan. It was almost cartoon-funny to see the Barmy Army looking perplexed as Nat led them in a chant for our goalie, Faye Baker, but Faye and the team were delighted, and so was I. I was also delighted when the Army (albeit briefly) sang, 'From the banks of the Irwell to the shores of Sicily, we will fight, fight, fight for Lewes FC', instead of the usual 'United FC'. What an honour! Charlie and the fans in our box were incredulous.

I felt a little eccentric at first – a wide-brimmed red hat can make you stick out at a football match – but then I generally felt a little out of place at matches back then anyway, and the fedora's conspicuousness publicly reflected something of that feeling. So

---

19 Gary The Badge is a longstanding Lewes fan who sells football club badges from a wide variety of clubs just inside the turnstiles at the Dripping Pan. His real name is Gary.

I simply became braver and owned it. Fake it to make it? Always been pretty sound advice.

On the pitch we put on a good show, which everyone agreed was not really reflected by the 5–0 defeat. When Shannon entered the players' lounge afterwards, though, she was fuming. 'I told her to check out her eyelashes before she fouls me again!' she announced, talking about Alex Greenwood, Lioness. Shannon's own face was also made up, as it usually was on a matchday, or any other day of the week. Again, the juxtapositioning of these strong, physical women with their make-up was a situation I very much enjoyed. There were no frail females here, but that didn't mean they had to ape men and show up in a masculine way. I mean, fine, if that's what they wanted to do, but, you know, equally fine if they didn't. The message that repeatedly came through to me via women's football went against all that lazy, restrictive stereotyping and was one of inclusivity – just 'do you' and you will be accepted and welcomed here. Phew! A great relief! And this was a lesson I was continually learning for myself, in or out of a red fedora.

If I felt a little out of place at matches sometimes, once on the board I felt more and more like a space invader. It was as if I was gradually edging in on other people's territory and making them uncomfortable as well as myself. Again, I wouldn't quite describe the feeling as 'imposter syndrome', however – that feeling that many people (especially women or those from a minority background) have about not being good enough for their job even though they're absolutely qualified to be there.

I could see that I was producing results, and felt confident in my difference. I believed myself to be an asset to the board, even if the board might not all have wholeheartedly agreed, even questioning the relevance of what I was doing at times ('What exactly is the purpose of the SisterShips?', 'You're introducing a suffragette film at the local cinema on behalf of the club – why?', etc., etc.). As I spent more time at board meetings and on our internal Slack channel, debating various decisions and imparting information, it was clear that not every director was strongly behind some of the equality messaging. Or thought much about its importance to our growing brand. Or even about our growing brand, for that matter. And it was clear that I – not a fan of men's football, with my strong sense of mission and feminist leanings – wasn't always entirely welcome.

So I did feel I was an imposter all right, but I felt it was a *good* thing! A powerful thing even. And a real thing – not an imagined identity stemming from a lack of self-esteem. I remember, though, that when we moved into lockdown in 2020 and all our meetings were on Zoom, my confidence waned. There were some big personalities and dominant voices on the board, and some who liked to display their football knowledge while totally ignoring my 'impact' work, which usually took place off the pitch. I felt unseen and sometimes excluded. It got to the stage where I stuck a Post-it note to my screen saying, 'You belong in this room' (thanks to the writer Viv Groskop for that, and her podcast *How to Own the Room*), just to reassure myself in the presence of 'football people'.

I was finding that confidence was everything, and that many of the men I worked with in football seemed to have it in spades. So I learned from them, faking it to make it a little more, appreciating my good fortune at being in a position where I could pick up tips from these unusual (to me) people. Many of my new male colleagues and fellow fans displayed, for example, the kind of innate confidence and passion that allowed them to think they were better than the manager when it came to footballing decisions. It was the writer Sarah Hagi who said, 'Lord, give me the confidence of a mediocre white man.' I'd adjust that to 'Lord, give me the confidence of a male football fan shouting coaching instructions at his team.' I mean it when I say that I was supremely grateful to these men for their example. I could see that I had a choice on the board of directors – speak up about your experience and share your opinion, or dissolve into shyness and affect very little. The writer Chimamanda Ngozi Adichie has written eloquently about how women are taught to 'make ourselves smaller', so it wasn't the easiest thing for me to do, but I chose pretty early on to speak out.

So, I learned from my environment, adapting somewhat to be effective while also striving to keep valuing my difference. It was a tricky tightrope to walk – fitting in enough to be respected and influence change while staying different enough to avoid conventional thinking. Too weird (friendly, open, emotional, off-topic) and I risked disrespect and mistrust on the board. Too 'footbally' (though, realistically, what were the chances?!) and I risked losing my willingness to suggest off-the-wall stuff. I often worked on unusual projects for the club – ones I knew would help more outsiders (like 'unwelcome women') feel welcome while also contributing to both my own and Lewes FC's growth. In fact, I saw parallels between my own journey and that of Lewes FC. Here we both were, playing with the 'big boys' (hello, Man U; how's it going, Aston Villa; hi there, Crystal Palace) and relying on our difference and radical – for football – nature to stay there and create value through the difference.

For most of 2020's lockdown, football held its breath. Players stowed away their boots, clubs worried about the lack of revenue and stadiums became empty shells. I decided to write us a ten-point diversity and inclusion action plan, convinced that nurturing diversity would lead us to make better business decisions in a difficult climate (while also making me feel more at home). We needed to make decisions that led to innovation so that we could wring the most out of our relatively small (compared to the women's teams attached to men's Premier League sides that we were up against) budget. Our independent brand stood out, and we were doing well in attracting sponsors and new owners. But to stay relevant and be in with the chance to get the women into the Super League, we needed to perform even better commercially.

Chapter 16
A Town Called Fuckery

Forgive me my nonsense, as I also forgive the nonsense of those
who think they talk sense.

Robert Frost

In the process of writing this book, I realised that I turned 50 in 2017 – the same year I fell hostage to gender equality in football. I know now that I was perimenopausal – or, to put it politely, 'getting ready to assert myself in ways I hadn't before'. You could also say 'fed up with putting up with shite', or 'on the verge of smashing up my home sometimes if no one emptied the dishwasher'. In addition, President Trump was in power in America for most of my time at Lewes FC, espousing a clear view that women should submit to his belief about their social function in the world, and men should be free to indulge in 'locker room talk'. Moreover, Boris Johnson was prime minister in the UK for at least half of my board term and was called out in an ITV documentary[20] for presiding over a 'nasty, misogynist culture' while in power. Our PM reportedly brought with him 'a very masculine culture . . . you know, lads down the pub', hosted a party at Downing Street where a 'Sexist of the Year Award' was handed out and, according to an anonymous young woman said to have worked there and interviewed for the documentary, 'if you were a female in that sort of zone, it was actually quite uncomfortable to work in'. By every criterion I could think of, women's rights globally were getting worse.

This explains a lot as I look back on stunts like suffragette flash mobs and how willing the participants were, or having the gall to speak publicly, be interviewed on TV at the drop of a hat, act as a radio pundit despite a lack of knowledge, put myself forward to be elected to a football club board, insist a female pirate statue was a good idea for a football ground,[21] and be what many have now generously called 'the best kind of Karen'. Mouthy maybe, insistent perhaps, all over social media sometimes, yes, a 'doer', a director, a pain in the arse for some, I know, but – however annoying I may have been – advocating on behalf of the disaffected and trying to change things up. Because, of course, I'd had a full half-century of the way things are and, like many other menopausal women I know, there was a rage inside me.

It was just two years after the introduction of gender equality to football that menopause hit proper. I tend to relate to the

20 Tonight: Boris Johnson: The Rise and Fall.
21 See Chapter 17 for the story of *Inexorable*.

cultural anthropologist Margaret Mead on this: 'There is no more powerful force in the universe than a menopausal woman with zest.' (Of course, Mead is more famous for another quote, which, it is fair to say, also applied at Lewes FC: 'Never doubt that a small group of thoughtful committed individuals can change the world. In fact, it's the only thing that ever has.')

So now, a full year into my board role, aged 52 and *fully* menopausal, I did the obvious thing during lockdown, and invented a town called Fuckery. It was inspired by the lyrics of one of my favourite Amy Winehouse songs, and saved my sanity when things got intense on that board. Fuckery was a place I could send anyone and everyone when they annoyed me. Yes, it existed only in my head, but knowing it was there meant I could remain pacific on the outside. 'Oh yes, play their game!' howled the fierce, hormone-beguiled, insomniac, tired-but-wired, overwhelmed, righteously furious, proud witch within me; while my *own* game – the town of Fuckery – stopped me from writing overlong messages of defiance on the directors' Slack channel or – God forbid – Facebook. I didn't speak too loudly in board meetings, or *scream*, because Fuckery was there, waiting patiently to accommodate any total numpties, the perfect place for virtual banishment. To be clear, it was a godforsakenly annoying town where people effed everything up and excelled at it. And when anyone I encountered needed to make the journey to Fuckery, off they went, for a well-deserved stint of work in that useless place with their fellow nitwit residents.

With Charlie's willing help, I frequently sent various of my fellow board members to the hotel in Fuckery for a temporary stay, when remaining in sane communion with them would otherwise have been difficult. Some people would earn provisional roles there, and only returned home when they'd a*$ed everyone about enough at that infuriating establishment. Someone would become the receptionist in the hotel, sending everyone to the wrong rooms, of course, because they 'didn't think it was a priority' to check. Someone else would become town crier of Fuckery, and only shout about the most trivial stuff related to the minutiae of *men's* football, with never a word on the women's game. Someone else might become mayor for a while, because they liked being in charge but got absolutely sweet FA done. One unsuspecting colleague became MP for Fuckery but then failed to turn up to important meetings where they were needed to vote. Someone else became hotel manager for some weeks, putting obstacles galore in the way of getting a new initiative off the ground, so that no innovation could ever be introduced at that decrepit house of lodging. As for the pub – well, the staff messed up the orders, miscounted the till takings and were known for terrible customer service. All par for the course in Fuckery, where nothing useful was ever achieved. This – extreme and admittedly unreasonable – visualisation technique provides limitless fun in its detailing (don't be afraid to write down what people say and wear, what they promise and fail at, the nuanced default male phrasing of their conversations), and I recommend it to any woman going through menopause while being mansplained to, himterrupted, or just plain over-effing-looked at work.

Fuckery is your answer.

In fact, this advice is likely health-promoting to many women over 45 years of age who need to be strategic about reining things in, staying calm and carrying on, whether in football or not. It's hard when you're angry. Listen, I even had to send *myself* there once or twice, landing myself a job as a doormat waitress or a useless shop-window dummy. Usually because I hadn't been assertive enough, and what I should have said was keeping me awake at 3 a.m. Alongside the odd menopausal sweat, of course.

Back when I was counselling, we talked about 'presenting problems'. These are the issues clients arrive with, when there is really another issue that the presenting one is covering up. It's just that the presenting one is more acceptable in their life than the real one: it's the one they can admit to. Men often come to a therapy session angry with someone or something, and the therapist may facilitate them to reach into the anger and beyond, where sadness often waits – an emotion that men are traditionally trained not to express. It can really shift the client's outlook to express that sadness in a completely accepting environment. Whereas a woman may arrive crying and clearly sad, but when we delve deeper, she is also angry, and those tears are covering sheer unexpressed rage, a rage that it's often cathartic to explore. I found the menopause to be like a bloody-minded therapist who gave me full permission to feel my anger. And here I was, in an environment full of unconscious male privilege, being triggered almost daily. I had to feel it, and I *really* had to laugh at it too!

The greatest benefit of my unlikely combination of menopause and football, though, was that I became less self-conscious, and less inclined to look after people. You *could* say that 'good girl' no longer, I became a b*tch. You'd be wrong, though. You see, I noticed that men generally weren't looking at me as a potential sexual partner any longer. And until they left off, I hadn't realised how often they *had* done, and how being conscious of it had somehow stifled my voice and undermined me. No longer! Now I felt more freedom. I could, you know, say my piece, without spoiling some man's fantasy! I'm laughing as I write, but, however ludicrous it sounds, it's true. I didn't have to 'look after' men any more. This insight seemed to arrive with my diminished visibility, in the world as an older woman, my building of Fuckery, and the development of the – very beautiful – quality of 'fuck it'. A characteristic you could also call 'resolve'. And now here I was, a football club director. I had entered the citadel of the very thing I'd hated just a couple of short years ago – by way of *feminism*, of all things – and lo, my menopause was my secret weapon. I didn't care about egos, I was fed up of talking, I just wanted to get things done. Fuck it!

While on the subject of menopause, I should mention the fans. Not *football* fans. It was in 2021 that Charlie decided to make manifest the club's hashtag, #FansOfChange, in material form, designing some actual hand-held fans, the kind you wave in front of your face to cool yourself down. On their red and black folds they bore the message 'Fans of Change', alongside our logo. Made sustainably from bamboo, these were handy gifts at speaking engagements, or for sponsors, or visitors we were hosting at the Pan. And they were particularly welcomed by menopausal women. I even have a recent picture of Davina McCall holding one at an event that Lewes FC's commercial manager, Stef McLoughlin, and I attended in 2023 about the menopause. Once again Lewes FC was manifesting its brand in a clever and relatable way. Do you know another club that reaches out to menopausal women with witty merch? No?

Say no more. And in case you're wondering, there are no fans of change in Fuckery.

Chapter 17
Making It Up As We Go Along

The only ground you can eat hummus in the terraces
and not be laughed at.

British Football's Greatest Grounds

'Out of ten duck-sized horses and one horse-sized duck, who would win in a fight?' New Zealand international striker and vegan activist Katie Rood and I are on the commuter train from Lewes to Victoria. It's 2019 and we're killing time as we travel to Channel 5 News in London to talk about the history of women's football and the imminent World Cup.

'I don't know. I reckon on the horse-sized duck?' I venture. The absurd conversation develops into a consideration of which would be the more friendly companion, and the relative difficulty of clearing up horse manure versus the pleasure of being able to ride the duck.

Katie signed for Lewes FC Women fresh from Juventus (a team even *I'd* heard of) in Italy. As she was new to Lewes, and in need of a bit of help with the culture, I'd taken her under my wing, showing her around town. As the club grew in reputation, we were attracting players from way beyond our previous south coast/south London catchment area, and some of these young women, coming to England from abroad, leaving family and friends behind them, needed a support structure. The club wasn't quite set up to provide this yet, so basically Katie got me!

'Roodie' was not only a fans' favourite on the pitch, she was also a brilliant communicator off it, on a mission to change the world. We did assemblies and talks, and appeared on national TV together opining on Equality FC, World Cups, players using their voices, social justice and the environmental impact of football. One way or another we spent a lot of time in each other's company, and I learned close-up about the very real rigours and difficulties of a female international athlete's life. Roodie was particularly well placed at Lewes. She was vocal about change, and passionately activated for the rights of women footballers, animals and the planet itself. We could rely on her to be articulate in front of a mic, but crucially, she was also mature enough to be empathic about the tone to adopt with different audiences. Katie Rood was a fully rounded, purpose-driven human being, not put off by the limelight. An absolute gift for Lewes FC!

As with Shannon, Roodie and I had some adventures together representing the club at various events, and I was very grateful to them both for their inclusive attitude towards me – something I didn't always come across from other women already immersed in football. There were times when it felt that women who had been in football (men's or women's) for some years, or all their lives, were a little less than welcoming. I came to appreciate that women in football were a small group back then, and most of them seemed to know, or know of, each other. I, on the other hand, was a Joanna-come-lately, turning up and talking to anyone who'd listen about this 'new' product. Maybe they found me a little annoying, or intimidating, or odd. I wouldn't be surprised; I'm sure I was!

Again, I was careful not to let the notion of exclusion be a problem, but to continue with the mission to raise the profile of the women's game among a new market who would support it. If we weren't on the telly, Roodie and I were talking in London pubs to local branches of the Women's Equality Party, or doing school assemblies. She even encouraged me to become vegan for a few weeks (and to this day I still eat more plants because of a striker from New Zealand). Doubtless, though, the respect and friendship of an athlete lent me some credibility – towards myself as much as anyone else! I regularly talked to people about women's football and footballers, and here was a real-life fully professional one, who had represented her country on the world stage, played for a top internationally competitive team and trained, ate and lived for football, backing up every word I said with her lived experience. *And* she was in the FIFA 19 computer game, a fact that impressed many a cross-legged little boy looking up at her from the floor in the primary schools we visited together!

Being an imposter-without-a-syndrome-about-it in football, it was water off a duck's back for me to introduce Roodie to Gary Lineker at a book signing in London, for example, and grab a photo of her while brightly telling the former player and popular presenter that they were 'two strikers together'. I happily reminded Gary that when we'd met before – at a festival, when I'd also doorstepped him about Lewes FC – he'd promised to come and watch a Lewes FC Women's match . . . and hadn't. Roodie found my easy manner with Lineker very funny. Why not? To me, men's football wasn't the venerated subject it was for some. She also found it amusing that when she showed me a picture of 'the most famous footballer in the world' on the train on the way back to Lewes, to 'test' me, I could neither recognise nor name him (he's called Ronaldo). I was conspicuously unfazed by men's football, unembarrassed by my ignorance. I felt it to be a big ego-driven business that didn't need any more worship or star-struckness than it already got! And Roodie was brilliant at advocating for the resources that women footballers needed to be able to play with dignity and respect. It's also true, though, that as the seasons went on, I became a fan of Lewes FC Men, and grew to understand the interesting cultural differences in football, and its environments, at different levels and genders of the game.

Roodie raved to me about the musical talent of her flatmate, Jess King, another Lewes striker, who was a spoken word and rap artist. Liverpudlian Jess had previously played abroad, and told me a sorry story about a boot sponsor at a club refusing to give boots to the women, and then declining to even let the women *buy* any boots from them saying they were 'only for the men'! She was defiantly angry about the sexism she had regularly encountered. So, we hatched a plan. Roodie asked Jess to write a song about gender inequality in football. Jess obliged in a matter of hours. Charlie and I introduced her to our friend Max, a local music producer, and we released 'Raise Us Up' in 2019. Our then kit sponsors, Kappa, kindly kitted her out ('It's like Christmas!' she exclaimed on seeing the box of goodies they'd given her), and I took the promo photographs, while Charlie shot the video. We were hopeful Jess's track would do well, but unfortunately, with no contacts in the rap world, it didn't go far. I encourage anyone reading this to have a look at YouTube, because 'Raise Us Up' is a buzzy anthem for female footballers, in which Jess sends a strong and catchy message to football federations around the world.

Meanwhile, that same year, Hasbro brought out a new version of their famous game, Monopoly. In 'Ms Monopoly', women got paid more than men for passing Go, and all the properties are inventions created by women. It immediately brought to mind something Roodie had said to me after one of our public talks together: 'Karen, given all the things you listed about previous lack of resources, time spent training, and us being in the Championship and the men in non-league – shouldn't we actually be getting *more* than the men's team, rather than the same?'

'Woah!' I'd answered. 'Hold your duck-sized horses, Katie! Do you know how many conversations, how much convincing it's taken just to get to *equality*? Now you're talking about *equity* – paying each gender what they need in order to have an equal opportunity in the context of their playing environments – and that's a few seasons away!' But we both knew she was absolutely right.

I wrote to Hasbro to ask if we might have 45 sets of Ms Monopoly to give our players as presents. They kindly obliged! I don't know if the players experienced the kind of squabbling we did round our kitchen table, with our daughter getting more than our son as they passed Go. But hey, it's always worth experiencing the world from another point of view, isn't it? Roodie liked the game anyway!

Also in 2019, something amazing happened. England's Lionesses broke viewing records when they reached the semi-finals of the World Cup. They put women's football centre stage that summer, and the country got behind them, many watching the women's game on TV for the first time. Gratified, I wrote a passionate article for HuffPost about why we should see these women as role models for our children, rather than the *Love Island* contestants whose dramas were playing out at the same time on the other channel. The article went viral on social media. I was attending an event at the Houses of Parliament with Roodie when an MP asked whether I'd read the HuffPost piece. 'She wrote it!' replied Roodie, quick as a flash. We had a laugh, sensing Lewes FC's growing influence.

As the club's unique profile and 'disruptor' reputation grew, and with our women in the Championship and our Isthmian League men's crowds increasing too, we attracted more attention and more great people to the club. This was of course part of a cunning plan often spoken about by Ed and Charlie to develop Lewes FC into 'an exemplary football club on the largest achievable stage'. With an extended footballing platform, we reached a bigger audience for our messages of equality. Attracting more owners and sponsors with those messages would put money back into our playing budgets – a virtuous circle.

The 'moon-shot'[22] mission was taking off. Directors on the board were increasingly busy, and time became even more of a precious resource. So, as required by the FA, in August 2019, we appointed a new general manager for the women's team. It was a special appointment that involved directors wooing one Maggie Murphy to move to Lewes from London and take on the full-time role. Maggie came from a human rights and advocacy background but had been a keen footballer from a young age, even – coincidentally – playing for an Isle of Wight team against Lewes at the Dripping Pan back in the eighties. She had co-founded an organisation called Equal Playing Field, championing gender equality in sports and organising stunts to draw attention to inequalities.

I'd met Maggie at the All-Party Parliamentary Group that Shannon and I had attended, and also at a meeting at the Twitter HQ in London, and then again at a special screening of a documentary about a group of female footballers (including Maggie) climbing Kilimanjaro to play the world's highest-altitude match in order to make a point about the mountains women have to scale to get a fair deal in football. Was fate throwing her into Lewes FC's orbit? As a board, we believed Maggie would be perfect for the job and the club at this stage of its development:

---

22 'Moon shot' was the term used by Ed to describe the ambitious and groundbreaking mission to propel Lewes FC Women into the Super League. And when they asked, 'But how did "Little Lewes" do that?', the club could say, 'We were powered by gender equality'. And do a mic drop.

she knew football, had connections in the game, and was a seasoned organiser, advocate and communicator. We felt she'd be more than capable of handling the task ahead. In turn, she was delighted to work for a club she was so intrigued and impressed by, and of which she was already an owner. Employing Maggie was a huge move for us as a board, and a big deal for her too, as she uprooted from London to Lewes.

We also employed Lynne Burrell – previously a volunteer at the club attracted by the welcome on matchdays – ahead of the 2019–20 season, to do the bookkeeping under Ed's guidance. We had another change of manager on the women's side when Fran left to coach the women's team at Celtic in Scotland and his assistant, Simon Parker, took over.

On the board, Maggie organised our work into pillars, and we agreed a clear strategy for each one. The pillars were 'Full Financial Sustainability', 'Our House in Order', 'Fan and Community Engagement', 'Quality Winning Football' and 'Impact on the World'. Although engaged across a few pillars, I led on the club's 'Impact on the World'. On this pillar, Charlie innovated with our campaigning for equal prize money in the FA Cup, eventually creating the calculator mentioned earlier for fans to work out how much better (or in a tiny percentage of cases, worse) off their club would be under our new, fairer system. Director John Peel worked alongside Ed on anti-gambling activations, collaborating with charities and working to dissociate football from its over-association with gambling, with particular reference to kids, so vulnerable to influence by the game, believing because of the pervasiveness of gambling advertising in football that gambling was simply a fun and harmless thing to be doing. The number of clubs who *still* allow role models to wear shirts with betting sponsors all over them is depressing, and another clearly irresponsible message that football has allowed to become the norm.

For my part, working on the inclusion of women and girls, it helped tremendously to *be* a woman, and, moreover, one who hadn't known much about football and its culture but who *was* into art, literature, fashion, feminism, psychology, parenting, etc. – things that other women who didn't like football (yet) might be into. Also helpful were my increasing resolve, the creation of Fuckery, and the authority my role on the board gave me as I leaned into it more and more. I got cracking.

I expedited the creation of breastfeeding signs, for example, and an area where people could feed babies privately at matches if they wanted to. This followed an approach from our steward, Rosie Watts. Again I was struck by how important it is to have women in positions of authority at the ground, because other women go and speak to them, and unlike the male stewards, a female steward had thought twice about suggesting you go and feed your baby in the toilets! Likewise, it is important to have women in decision-making positions, because thus Rosie knew she could come to me and that I would empathise enough with the request to take positive action. Of course, this isn't to put men down. It's to recognise that many of us, by virtue of our life experiences, have different mental priorities, and that for too long, footballing environments have grown around the priorities of straight white middle-aged men. Believe me when I say that I had the breastfeeding sign very intentionally placed at the front of the ground, so that it is the first thing you see when you walk through the turnstiles. This isn't necessarily because we have flocks of parents wondering where to go to feed their kids (though we do have some); rather it is a clear indication to away fans of the kind of club we are. We do not expect all our visiting fans to be people *without* babies to care for. Another conscious signal.

I introduced free sanitary towels and pads in the women's toilets, having worked with an excellent organisation called the Red Box Project, which collected sanitary products for girls at school. It was properly gratifying to think that a 14-year-old girl could come along to a Lewes FC Women's (or Men's) match for free – all under-16s go free at Lewes – watch her elite athlete role models play football, and get a free sanitary product in the toilet should she need one. What a brilliant no-cost afternoon out! We were proud of this offer, especially given that the away clubs I now visited on Saturdays for men's matches really didn't seem to be considering 14-year-old girls on their periods. But then neither were they particularly thinking about breastfeeding mums, dads who needed somewhere to change their babies, or kids exposed to gambling hype from club sponsors.

I also requested non-dairy milk alternatives in all our food outlets, having been disappointed by a lack of oat or soya milk for tea at away matches, and knowing that some of our new market would feel the same way. Why couldn't we get tea and coffee the way we liked it just 'because it's football'? It's so *easy* to provide another milk option.

I applied for a grant from the town council for hoardings around the pitch with feminist and anti-gambling quotes on them – it was very important to me to define our ground as the home of Equality FC and a place where change was being actively campaigned for. I knew that I wouldn't be involved in football if it wasn't for the equality campaign, and that therefore I wouldn't be involved with any other football club. This one needed to display the right *visual* signals for me to feel properly welcome, and to be a place I could show guests around and be proud of. Calling the project No Place Like Home, I knew that if *I* felt at home, others who eschewed football because it had never been given to them might feel the possibility of belonging too. One of my pitch boards is a quote from Mary Wollstonecraft, which reads, 'I do not wish women to have power over men; but over themselves.' I don't think you'll find that kind of perimeter board at many other football clubs.

Within the 'Impact on the World' group, and with the support of members of the SisterShips, I took on various projects that were to further challenge me both professionally and personally. Not all of them ended in success (I never did get Chanel to sponsor us with their Rouge Noir range, for instance), but some did. For example, during the pandemic period, Charlie and I spotted a BBC news story about a Devon council rejecting an eight-foot statue of Anne Bonny and Mary Read – bisexual female pirates from the 18th century – on the grounds that it was 'inappropriate' and they'd rather have 'a fisherman and his wife and some pilchards'. This was another opportunity to define ourselves. I tweeted the sculptor, Amanda Cotton, saying that if Devon didn't want the pirates, Lewes did, and we'd be honoured to offer them a home at the Dripping Pan.

After some toing and froing about transportation costs, positioning, insurance and our ethos, Amanda gifted us the awesome piece, until such time as it should be requested by an appropriate seaside location. I got a small grant from a local arts fund to cover those transportation costs (*Inexorable*, weighing in at a ton of marine concrete, was currently at the docks in east London), and it wasn't too long before our pirates were being swung over the old flint wall of the Pan from a crane-loaded truck as Amanda and I watched nervously. (A bit of Anne Bonny's hair is probably still in Mountfield Road to this day; it chipped off as she moved horizontally over the wall, not quite clearing the top. Try as we might, we never could find that rock of a lock!) Anne and Mary now stand tall by the chip hut, for all to see and read about. Indeed, you can even buy 'Pirate Fries' at the time of writing – seaweed mayonnaise has become a thing at the Pan.

We welcomed the arrival of *Inexorable* by growing sea buckthorn around it – the excellent suggestion of volunteer Michael Kennard. And as per Amanda's wish, the women face the pitch, where they 'watch' matches but also look in the direction of the sea, not *too* far away from us in Lewes. I threw a launch party for the statue, where sea shanties were sung, rum consumed, and various marine-related guests invited – people who might not otherwise have dreamed of coming to the Pan. I've since enjoyed introducing many fans and guests to Anne and Mary, saying, 'They're not exactly role models, because, you know, they *were* ruthless and violent, but just like female footballers, they invaded male territory and were wildly successful, and not enough people know about them.' Amanda – now a Lewes FC fan, of course – has creatively expressed the women's stories and personalities, from Anne's flyaway hair to Mary's thrashing scars, in the forms she has sculpted. I, for one, stand up taller every time I pass the statue, and let's face it – it's a great story.

However, in case any of this is sounding too easy, I should mention that, well . . . it wasn't. One owner and long-term fan said that the statue was 'the last straw' and he'd be rescinding his ownership forthwith. Another local owner was so upset that the club was 'spending money on statues and not putting it into playing budgets' that he called for board resignations. Comments such as these were diligently replied to – 'The last straw of what?', 'No money that could have been spent on football was spent on the statue – it was a gift transported here via an arts grant' – and conversations entered into. In fact, conversations with owners happened all the time, whether in person at matches, online in virtual 'town halls', on social media, by email or even in the local supermarkets.

In 2021, new directors joining the board included three more women, and we promoted Maggie to CEO and Lynne to general manager, so that the club could professionalise with proper staff, and volunteer elected directors might transition to be less 'hands-on', so making the club more sustainable long-term. That was the plan, anyway!

Maggie was an organiser par excellence who restructured our ways of working, while Lynne took on the management of women players' lives off the pitch and the headache of arranging fixtures (plus a hundred other things as well). It's difficult to overstate how diligently both women worked in these roles, and how many hours they devoted to the club. It also felt necessary for many of us – including the volunteers who contributed time and expertise in such a wide variety of areas – to be giving extra hours to the club. If you can imagine, we were acting like a start-up organisation that was not only responsible for putting on or participating in over 50 live events a year – some of which attracted more than a thousand, even two thousand people – but was also an impactful campaigning body trying to change the world. We gave ourselves a lot of work, but the cause felt justified.

For season 2021–2, we had new managers for our men's team in the form of Tony Russell and assistant Joe Vines. This was a boon for Equality FC. Both men came into a club which was already practising equality and were completely aligned with the ethos. I had heard from other directors that men's non-league football sometimes harboured a shady culture of bullying and speaking to players in an 'old school' (read: disrespectful) way. But these two men were very keen on openness and respect and wanted the men's team to be included in the club's equality messaging. Upon joining Lewes, Tony overtly stated that he would ensure 'that we play with the same integrity and values that the club has established off the pitch'.[23]

And the good people kept on coming. I found myself helping facilitate the establishment of our community garden that year, as envisioned and created by men's midfielder Bradley Pritchard. This was another unusual addition to our ground, made possible by the club's reputation for serving its community. Pritchard, an ex-pro player, also a trained human rights lawyer and an educator and facilitator of young people, had signed to the men's side on the condition he could set up a community garden, having previously created one near his home in south London. Tony and Joe agreed this with the board, and since I lived nearby and worked on our impact, I stepped in. These men were all groundbreakers (Bradley in the literal sense too, as he turned 'grey' land green), bringing innovation as well as a broad and sympathetic understanding of the relative positions of men's and women's football in the wider game as a whole. This perception of the club's potential impact from the men's side was much appreciated by me, given some of the comments we still got from a small minority of Lewes FC Men's most ardent fans, who would declare that 'the club should stick to football', or casually talk about 'women's football' as opposed to '*normal* football'.

I arranged my first meeting with Bradley, and invited Biram Desai, our newly employed financial director, along too. Biram and I were the same age, and had already realised that we'd probably

23 Saturday, 24 April 2021, kentishfootball.co.uk.

attended the same London nightclubs in our twenties. This was enough to lead us to share an in-joke regarding board meeting minutes, which were always written up diligently by Biram. He deliberately inserted a weird phrase for me to spot every time, and I'd routinely contact him after each board meeting to see if I'd got it right. There was no prize when I did, but at least he knew *someone* was reading the minutes, and I enjoyed the camaraderie with someone who shared some of my past life experience (so important for an outsider like me to have some common reference points, even if it was just an underground nightclub in Paddington!).

Biram and I met Bradley in the Rook Inn clubhouse over a cup of tea, and I asked Bradley to articulate the vision and aims of the garden, intending both a press release and a call for volunteers to come from this meeting. He was inspirational as he talked about his ideas. His clear willingness to roll up his sleeves and get on with it, coupled with his experience and energy, completely bowled us over. Enthused, I started to draft a vision statement, thinking about grants and sponsorships for such a fantastic project. Bradley looked worried, saying, 'Slow down here, we need to manage expectations about what the allotment will be able to produce.' Boom! This comment reminded me of an old country song, so to show him that I understood, I sang, 'I beg your pardon, I never promised you a rose garden.' Biram maintained he'd never seen a footballer look quite so surprised on a first meeting with a club director.

I loved working with Bradley, and connecting him with various sustainability groups around town. He met expert local composter Michael Kennard (he of the sea buckthorn), who worked with him to bring composted soil and compost bins to the ground. It wasn't long before the two like-minded guys had transformed the south-east corner of the Dripping Pan. We started a self-regulating WhatsApp group of volunteers for the garden, and asked owners, in Lewes FC's weekly newsletter, what we should call the new space, explaining that it would contribute to our women's players' lunches and local food banks, and be a practical learning tool for 'growing good food and good relationships'. Director Trevor Wells and I had fun picking the winner. 'Brad's Pit' was the brainchild of a fan in the Netherlands and has stuck ever since. If I knew of a way to reach Hollywood star Brad Pitt and ask him to sponsor the garden, you know I would. Meanwhile, the allotment thrives, with a dedicated team of some 30 volunteers, and as an endless talking point among visitors who don't expect a vegetable garden within a football ground, mere metres from the actual pitch.

Volunteers run courses there, teaching people to compost, plant, grow and cook. Students with and without special educational needs from the nearby college have created a hibernaculum and planted fruit trees. Volunteer Anthony Kalume, from local community group Diversity Lewes, has plans for a gazebo where people can relax and read. And we have taken to bunching up vegetables to present to players of the match, making a beautiful (and completely intentional) visual for post-match presentations on the men's side in particular, as we soften football's hard-man image a little with community spirit and ribboned clusters of home-grown Welsh onions. And if it weren't the growing season, I'd stop at the local flower shop to buy a small hand-tied bouquet for Lewes FC Men's Player of the Match on the way to the ground (couldn't let cultivation constraints get in the way of breaking down a bit of toxic masculinity!). And, to add to the Dripping Pan's growing reputation for being welcoming to all folks, Brad's Pit even boasts a bug hotel.

Naturally, everyone on the board was delighted to hear that we'd been voted the number one ground to visit in a new coffee table book by football fan and author Mike Bayly. Well, delighted and surprised. Fans kept telling us that they loved coming to the Pan, but the *very best*?! Bayly had researched and written *British Football's Greatest Grounds: 100 Must-See Venues*, offering 'a bucket list of places to watch football in England, Wales and Scotland as chosen by fans across the world'. It turned out that the Dripping Pan had received the most votes from away fans, claiming the no. 1 spot, ahead of Old Trafford, Goodison Park and the rest! My favourite pull quote from our write-up was: 'It's the only ground you can eat hummus in the terraces and not be laughed at.' Something I have since tested, and can confirm: not a soul batted an eyelid.

Once again, we were beating much, much bigger and better-known brands purely because we were inclusive and different. The more I reflected on our club's journey and Equality FC, the more I realised that we led with our women, and the developing values of women's football as the game grew. As the seasons passed, and the sponsors, owners and matchday revenues increased, our female players had become fully pro, training during the day, while our men's team were still, necessarily, part-time. It's not surprising that the inclusive, joyful, welcoming, community-spirited values of women's football spilled over into the entire club, informing the men's side too (Tony Russell: 'It's an unreal football club, with the best people you could ever want to meet'; Joe Vines: 'a club that shares so many values that are close to my heart'), and allowing equality to really be, as it says on the pitch advertising board fronting the TV gantry, 'a rising tide that lifts all boats'.

My growing relationships with the SisterShips organisations gave rise to an invitation to design a leadership awayday at the Dripping Pan for female PCs at Sussex Police who had been identified as lacking the confidence to apply for sergeant roles (they had no shortage of male applicants). I'd not designed a course before, but design it I did. The day was full of diverse sessions, each using football to illustrate various lessons. A chanting workshop with Donna McPhail taught participants how to use their voice and own their space; a talk about Lewes FC's recent history from Charlie and Stuart was designed to inspire; a workshop with Maggie on knowing your personal value aimed to give participants authority and self-knowledge; a session with captain Rhian Cleverly on how to earn the respect of the changing room would provide motivation; Bradley would organise teamwork games, followed by sessions with a coach on developing resilience. We rounded the day off with lessons in actual leadership on the pitch, both useful and hilarious. This was a wonderful way to utilise our great people, as well as all the lessons learned in using football as a vehicle for change. Following positive feedback, we were able to use some of these lessons for other corporate awaydays too. Result.

If you're wondering about ducks and horses, I *think* we plumped for the horse-sized duck, but do check out Katie Rood's YouTube channel for the very well-considered answer.

Chapter 18
Call Him Out

Until men conduct ourselves differently,
none of this is gonna change.

Nish Kumar

Equality FC, huh? Well, it's one thing to empower women by closing the gender pay gap and resourcing them fairly, but there's a whole other side to the question of equality – and that involves the dominant party. Women becoming empowered and men taking responsibility for toxic masculinity seem to be two sides of the very same coin.

Back in March 2021, just before International Women's Day, a woman called Sarah Everard was abducted, raped, strangled and burned by a serving police officer when she was just trying to walk home. We learned that the police officer in question had been nicknamed 'the Rapist' by his colleagues at work because of his openly misogynistic jokes and attitude towards women. It was a high-profile case, followed by other high-profile examples of men's violence against women and girls. As I kept up with the social media of Lewes FC's SisterShips, the reading was depressing. The prevailing feeling was of hopelessness, with women talking to women with anger, sympathy and despair for the future. Looking at the posts and comments, I concluded that while all this gathering of women, this networking and this sympathising was necessary, it sadly wasn't going to change the world. We needed men to step up and act. Somewhere during this pondering, it occurred to me that I was a director of a football club (insert light-bulb emoji, and remember, this title was still sometimes hard to identify with!), with access to lots of men, including 25 or so definite male role models in the players. And this wasn't just any football club, but one committed to using football as a vehicle for social change, leading with a campaign on gender equality. Too perfect an opportunity to miss, surely?

I discussed with Charlie how the SisterShips were joining the dots between a culture where rape jokes had become normalised, misogynistic 'locker room talk' made permissible in the highest of places, and a society where one woman is murdered by a man in the UK every day. Our SisterShip Survivors Network reported a lack of belief in rape victims (in fact, just 0.62 per cent of prosecutions for rape involve false allegations, according to the CPS), while the charity Rise, also part of the group, reported rapidly increasing numbers of contacts for their domestic abuse services. The Girls Network was concerned about girls' fears for their own safety amid the 'rape culture' rife in secondary schools. Sussex Police – proudly committed to the UN Women's

HeForShe campaign – was worried about the confidence of female police constables in a national environment where thousands of male officers stood accused of sexual assault. In football itself, there were countless questionable examples of male 'talent' being let off the hook, loaned to other clubs, or ranks closing, in the face of sexual assault or allegations of abuse or violence against women.

As we talked, Charlie came up with Call Him Out, a new Lewes FC campaign designed to kick-start men into taking accountability for male violence against women and girls. We know that not all men are perpetrators of violence, we really do. But as women and girls were explaining on social media, we can never know *which* men are, so we must assume every man is capable of violence against us, and therefore every man has a role in taking responsibility for himself and his fellow men. Introducing this campaign, I shared on the board that as a woman I have never been able to walk alone at night without fearing slightly (sometimes massively) for my safety. I walk home in the dark only as a last resort, and then with keys clutched firmly in my fist, just in case. I sit next to other women on trains at night. I wear shoes I can move fast in. I do these things because I am a woman living in a society with an epidemic of male violence against women. I also shared that I'd been sexually harassed more times than I could count for generally existing as a woman, and that I linked that harassment to a cultural tone that could escalate to violence. Why, for example, could I not go about my day (admittedly this applied much more when I was younger) without comments on the street from men I didn't know?

After a short discussion, where board members were sympathetic and one or two of the male directors mentioned their own female relatives, the campaign was approved. We talked to Lewes FC Men's managers, Tony and Joe (both allies of the cause for gender equality), about it. It wasn't long before every member of Lewes FC Men had pledged publicly that they would call out misogynistic comments and behaviours in themselves and others when they realised, heard or saw them. After discussion, Charlie wrote a statement:

Football is powerful. Its influence goes beyond the pitch, and beyond the full-time whistle. And, for now, football is a majority male sport, in participation and watching it.

So what better place to take action against the epidemic of misogyny, sexism and male-on-female violence?

Because it's time, it's way beyond time, that men took personal responsibility for what all women have to endure, day in, day out. This is a problem for men to resolve, not women.

Lewes FC Men's team want to do something as a group and as individuals.

From today, when anyone in the men's team (and managers and coaches) hears or sees something said or done by a workmate, family member, friend or anyone they're with, that they feel is disrespectful, sexist or harmful in any way to a woman, whether she's there or not, they will speak to that man and they will #CallHimOut. That might make them feel uncomfortable. But nowhere near as uncomfortable as the women on the receiving end of every demeaning comment.

Our men's team are good guys, like so many men, but now is the time to take action. And that action will include each man also calling themselves out sometimes, by going back on an ill-judged comment, by saying, 'Sorry, I shouldn't have said that.' This is a decision that starts within each man, to be part of the solution and not part of the problem.

'What stuff should I call out? Who decides?' people (men) may ask. The answer is that each man will develop their own radar, their own code and will know, in their heart, when something needs to be called out.

This is something that every man can do, and it will make a difference to women's everyday lives.

Phew! Following the men's team's pledges, male Lewes FC fans and followers took up the baton, affirming their own intentions to call out misogyny and sexism, while female followers breathed sighs of relief that these intentions were out on a public platform (Twitter) – rays of hope amid the pervading darkness of male-on-female violence.

I organised free 'bystander training' sessions with SisterShip Survivors' Network for Lewes FC players, directors and coaches. We learned how to safely act when we heard or saw abuse taking place. We also got great feedback from the trainers, who told us we were one of the most gender-diverse and vocally participative groups they'd ever had. I left the training very keen to ask people to 'unpack' dodgy jokes, as advised. 'Just ask them to explain to you why it's funny,' the trainer said. 'It usually kills the ism for them, gets them to think.' I was also looking forward to the next 'Women's football is boring', or 'Why should they get the same, they don't get the revenue', because I was going to parrot my newly learned phrase, 'Oh, that's interesting, because I feel the exact opposite way', and have a conversation.

The plan, organised with directors, a player and the managers, was to have a few regular compulsory Zoom sessions for the men's players about calling out sexism and misogyny. We'd listen to them, get their feedback on #CallHimOut, explore their experiences of this kind of thing in their own lives and create content for further discussion. We imagined that we would talk about ideas of what it means to be a man as well as negative online influences, and that we'd deconstruct toxic masculinity together. Then we'd organise for the first-team players to talk to our under-18s boys' team about masculinity, and about rape culture in their schools, and they'd share experiences and thoughts. There would not be 'instructions', as Bradley Pritchard put it, 'but listening'. We all felt strongly that the men's team were role models and would have influence over the younger men and boys. Key stakeholders in the team were up for it. This kind of thing – sitting in a group, exploring feelings – felt totally natural to me as a trained counsellor, but I knew it might be a little 'out there' for men's football.

However, we needed a male director to lead it, and no one had the time. Everyone was up to their necks, and after a few false starts, with plans to go and talk to the men at training called off for one reason or another, the plan was abandoned. As I write this, I'm still determined to make it happen. One obstacle is that the squad changes every season, so we will be starting afresh with new communications, connections, awareness-raising and pledges.

What did happen, however, was that we got coverage in local newspapers and sports media. This resulted in our local Labour Party members and then our local (Green/Lib Dem) town council members deciding to pass motions for their male colleagues to partake in #CallHimOut. We were proud of this, and watched as the male town councillors of Lewes pinned red and black ribbons to their jackets at a council meeting in the town hall, pledging to call out misogyny and sexism following the example of the town's football club.

The truth was, we didn't get too many openly sexist or misogynistic incidents at the club itself. With our female CEO, a couple of female directors, lots of PR about gender equality and conversations and surveys about it for our ownership; it wasn't really an environment where sexism could rear its head. There was the sign about breastfeeding as you walked into the ground, the female bisexual pirates standing tall in one corner, pitch boards with feminist quotes on them, and several female stewards. Maggie and I chatted about it in a talk together once for John Lewis – another employee-owned organisation. She reported how her bottom was randomly mentioned by a male stranger in the Rook Inn and she gave him short shrift. I once had a wolf whistle from the terrace at half-time during a men's game. I stopped, turned and asked the away fan in question, 'Did you just wolf-whistle me?' He looked cowed and said yes. 'Did you want a conversation?' I asked, without smiling. He didn't, upon reflection, and I decided I didn't mind. Crucially, I was surprised – this sort of thing was unusual at the Pan – but even so, I felt able to choose my reaction, and made the wolf whistle unacceptable.

As I started to go to men's matches more often, both home and away, I felt more comfortable attending now that Tony and Joe were at the helm and knowing there were gems like 'Pritch' in the team. I saw striking differences in culture compared with the women's games. One was the less inclusive, more threatening environment at away matches. I really didn't enjoy being among away fans at Worthing, for example, who shouted homophobic insults at our defender Will because he wore his hair long. It felt unsafe to counter their shouting because there were more of them than there were of us, but it was really nasty jibing. It made me angry and motivated enough to call it out if I heard it at the Dripping Pan. Our captain at the time, Mitch Nelson, did the same, even stopping a match at the Pan once when he heard homophobic abuse. He may have been booked by the referee for it, but his managers and the club's senior leadership were unanimously behind him. When I told him how much I admired him for what he'd done, he said, 'Anyone would have done the same.' But I knew that they wouldn't have. These cultures are created by activations, leadership, representation, signs and symbols, and the stories we tell. We were continually creating a new narrative for football at the Pan, and we were all a part of it.

I found that I was usually the only woman in the directors' hospitality room at men's away matches. The other directors were usually kindly older men who had loved non-league football, or even played it, all their lives and I had to work hard at my small talk in order to chat at half-time over a cup of tea and a biscuit. I almost felt sorry for them when they assumed I knew what they were talking about with regard to the league's history, matches they'd attended or players I didn't know the names of. I tried to stick to the weather and everyone's health. It was different at the Dripping Pan, of course, with more of our own directors in hospitality and more female staff around. There I could bang on about issues of social justice while munching on my Wagon Wheel, with every cultural permission to do so!

One time, two away supporters at the Pan cornered me and said, 'Hey, your player there, he's gay, isn't he?' I'd actually had dinner with the player in question and his girlfriend, but that wasn't the point. I was flummoxed by the question, eyes no doubt glinting, thinking, *what the actual* . . . and eventually asked, 'What do you mean?'

'Look how he shaves bits off his eyebrows. What *real* man does that? He's got to be gay!'

I wasn't sure where to start, but I knew this needed a conversation, and I wasn't turning away – not after bystander training! I felt safe at the Dripping Pan – home supporters were all around – and this pair didn't seem dangerous, just ignorant (and, just hazarding here, possibly repressed about their own masculinity or sexuality).

'I don't get what you mean by "real man". And why's it important to you whether he's gay or not?'

They answered by giving examples of what a so-called 'real man' did and didn't do, including 'I bet he looks in the mirror before he goes out. What real man does that?'

I explained that I didn't agree with their interpretation, and that I thought the bottom line was that we were all human beings together. I told them that this was an inclusive place – that if it wasn't, I wouldn't be there – and that we expected our guests to be inclusive too. They took this in and, having been initially keen to talk, shuffled away.

I wasn't happy, but I reminded myself that we're all on a journey, educating ourselves along the way. I'm not sure exactly what the right things to do and say are in these situations, but I know that first you have to keep yourself safe, and then I think it's good to have a conversation if you can, and question what is being said and why, explaining your own values as a club and as a person.

A diversity and inclusion consultant called Jiten Patel, whom I'd met on Zoom at an equality training course I'd signed up for, had given all of us on the board a free session on unconscious bias. It had reminded me of my counselling training – how to maintain positive regard and not make assumptions about people – and we'd had great feedback. Jiten generously worked pro bono with our coaches too. This kind of training really helps set the culture at an organisation, and it brought home the differences between men and women's football in terms of who is allowed to be themselves. I honestly never thought I'd be using lessons learned in therapeutic settings around the perimeter boards of a football club. But there we have it. We have to put down boundaries about what is and isn't acceptable and make sure there is an agreed vision. They don't agree? They need to go.

Full disclosure, it also reminded me of parenting lessons learned when we had the kids' friends around when they were young. You know the kind of thing: 'Yes, I understand you don't have to eat broccoli at home, but in *this* house we expect everyone to eat broccoli' (always said fairly firmly and followed by a bit of a walking-away flounce for good measure). As with broccoli, so with respect.

This was a pioneering journey for the whole club, and I was prouder by the day to be on it. Where else can you reach so many men and suggest change, other than in football?

Chapter 19
The Offside Rule and All That Jazz

———

Her wings are cut and then she is blamed
for not knowing how to fly.

Simone de Beauvoir

It's 2022, and I'm spending a fairly typical ten minutes messaging back and forth with apparently misogynistic men under an online article I've contributed to in a local paper, when I receive an exciting email from a local woman. So aligned is it with my mission at Lewes FC, so closely does it chime with my own experience of football, that I cannot wait to take action.

The keyboard warriors are asserting, with all the self-assurance in the world, of course, that women shouldn't be paid the same as men for playing football, that, it should be left to 'market forces' to decide their worth, and that, actually, nobody wants to watch women's football, do they? And in between long yawns and gulps of strong tea, I'm countering that men's football dominance was *artificially* created at a time when women's football was in fact attracting larger crowds than men's, and that the cultural and economic success of the men's game isn't the result of market forces but daylight robbery by the women's own FA, etc., etc. (honestly, it got tiring). So I was very much in the mood to do a bit more levelling of the playing field – this time off the pitch.

The email, from a woman named Julie, read:

> I started coming along to the women's matches a few years ago because I wanted to show my support for the pay parity. I am a woman in my 50s, was brought up being told that football was a boy's game and really it was not a part of my life. (Dad competed in motorbike events which – you guessed – I was allowed to watch but not ride!)
>
> Now I find myself loving Lewes FC, watching every women's home game and last year becoming an owner. But I have to confess to not being confident about the rules or strategies and tactics being used.
>
> I wondered whether the club could organise an evening for people like me who would like to know more about the game. A relaxed, informal event in the bar perhaps? Explaining the offside rule (again!?!).

So Julie has effectively been told, like so many women, to 'be careful'. It is for boys and men to be adventurous and take risks (motorbike riding), and of course, football – that well-known boys' club – is for men. But like many of us now in Lewes, she's tried a women's match in solidarity with gender equality and become a fan. The problem is, she doesn't know the rules or how to interpret what she's watching.

Of course! We had taught women to chant, but somehow expected them to simply follow the game and immediately grasp the rules of play! I'd forgotten how much football privilege I now had, with so many people around me, from fellow board members to coaches and injured players, to tell me what was going on and why. I'd asked *loads* of (*really* basic!) questions about the game over recent years, and could now tell you about types of formations, admire a good nutmeg, give you examples of 'set pieces', and talk about what constituted different kinds of foul. I'd even had Katie Rood explain the offside rule to me on a Southern Rail train table using various parts of a vegan dinner from Leon's. Most of the carriage was involved in our conversation by the end of the journey. It seemed men *really* wanted to explain this rule when they heard two women talking about it. Hilarious! I let them know as soon as was politely possible that Roodie had played for her country, and Juventus, and was now a striker at Lewes, and that I was quite happy with her explanation, thanks all the same. Their faces. Their interest! We'd had some fun train journeys.

Thanks to Julie, at the next board meeting I said I'd like to start a regular evening called 'The Offside Rule and All That Jazz', especially for fans new to the game, who in our case were likely to be (though not necessarily) women. Now, quite often on the board, when I mentioned a new Impact initiative (which I frequently did), I'd get a slightly uninterested response from some of the men. No objections as such, but not the amount of enthusiasm I'd have hoped for. This time, it seemed that most of the board wanted to actually help! 'You need football knowledge? I'm your man!' Eyes around the table had noticeably lit up! Board members were volunteering to come down to the Rook Inn and help me out, by explaining the offside rule to a new audience! I was both flabbergasted and amused by all this positivity.

At this point, though, I brought up the concept of 'mansplaining' and the potentially disempowering dynamic it could create if we had a man explaining the offside rule to a largely female audience. I don't know how many other football club boards have these kinds of discussions, but I'll bet not too many. The guys piped down, and we agreed that I'd ask members of the women's team to come and explain, and that I'd be careful to couch it as an evening of demystification where no question would be too silly. It was too easy for women to blame themselves for not understanding the rules, when they'd never been steeped in the kind of culture that afforded them the time or expertise to learn them. Or for men on Twitter to misogynistically claim that women inherently didn't understand the game and couldn't, for example, commentate on it. As well as fans and owners, I'd invite all the SisterShips organisations, as they were a good way to reach new supporters.

Before the first session, we dealt with a little social media feedback that we were being sexist by putting a picture of female fans up to advertise the evening, explaining that although 'The Offside Rule and All That Jazz' wasn't exclusively for women, it was women who made up most of our new audience (I can only imagine, though, how many times groups of male fans have been used to advertise football-related events, and how many – read few – times clubs have been called out for that!). Then, one dark, cold evening, I put red and black cushions I'd bought from IKEA on the (rather hard) seats in the Rook Inn, lit the room with some football-shaped lamps (also from IKEA), and introduced the sessions with a brief history of women's football, including the ban, and the narrative of Lewes FC's role in creating a more level playing field for women. Our women's captain, Rhian Cleverly (another player I'd loved doing talks with, and for ever 'Captain Pantastic' in my mind, after Charlie's spoof Elton John album cover matchday poster featuring her), answered questions humbly, clearly and revealingly, using a magnetic whiteboard and markers to show pitch positions and formations and talk the audience through set pieces. The evening went down a storm, with one woman saying she would now 'watch the match on Sunday through new eyes', which may just be one of my favourite pieces of feedback ever.

We continued the sessions, involving other players and female coaches, and the audiences (mixed gender, but mainly women) continued asking questions. As these became more specific, we started to 'theme' the evenings. Commercial manager Stef McLoughlin, who carried on organising the evenings, ran a brilliant one with particular emphasis on how the players' menstrual cycles affected play and training. This insight into the relationship between women's cycles and their physical and mental ability was revelatory (by 2023, Lewes FC Women had an app tracking their hormonal fluctuations, and giving them recommendations on eating, sleeping and the type of training to be doing according to their cycles), and it was brilliant to hear one of our older male fans asking questions about periods and saying, 'For the first time in my life, I feel permission to do so – thank you.' Framing discussions about women's hormonal health within football makes the subject far more accessible to some men.

At the time of that event, it was only the Lionesses, Chelsea FC and Lewes doing this kind of work. It was absolutely fascinating to our audience, and the kind of insight that brings fans closer to players, and frames women footballers as having specific needs and potential competitive edges that – because of the gender data gap – we are only just beginning to tap into. When we start healing those cut wings that Simone de Beauvoir alluded to with the resources needed to develop and explore women's gender-specific needs, we will watch as they soar. And if we carry on this way, women's football will go stratospheric over the next few years, both on and off the pitch.

Chapter 20
An American in Lewes

Diversity is being invited to the party; belonging is being
asked to dance.

Verna Myers, VP of inclusion strategy, Netflix

The more the club shouted about what we were doing off the
pitch, the more great people kept accepting that open invite to
join the movement. During 2021, with the increasing profile of
the women's game in clubs around us in the Championship and
above us in the WSL, the board recognised a strong need to
professionalise our women's side. The development was such that
we needed Lewes FC Women training every day, not just a couple
of days and a couple of evenings. We needed them supported by a
coaching team with not only strength and conditioning expertise,
but also nutritional, medical, well-being, mental and even
spiritual skills. Gradually players with full-time jobs, or those
who couldn't devote their time 100 per cent to their footballing
careers, were leaving the club.

On the board, we'd worked together to publish our strategy, and CEO Maggie had, as mentioned, organised the strategic goals into five operating pillars. We were each limited to working in two pillars to make workloads more realistic, but I straddled three because of the wide-ranging and joined-up nature of what I was doing. SisterShips, for example, came under 'Fan and Community Engagement', but also 'Impact on the World', and often led to commercial value within 'Full Financial Sustainability'. While leading on Impact, I regularly contributed to other pillars. I was minimally involved with the 'Our House in Order' pillar; I'd organised a disability survey, for example, with director Ed Briggs, who led that team, and I'd helped with HR work, which also fell into this area. In fact, at Ed B's suggestion I'd even organised for SisterShip friends Sussex Police to kindly bring us 14 seized marijuana lamps to help grow the grass around the dugouts, though in the end it was decided they would use too much electricity. However, I steered clear of the 'Quality Winning Football' pillar. The board still felt a pretty foreign place to me, and I stuck to what I knew, going with the flow when we were asked to vote on decisions involving player signings, etc. It wasn't as if I was twiddling my thumbs after all – there was a lot of work due to the hands-on nature of the board. Not only were we setting the vision and direction of the club, but without staff, other than our CEO, a facilities manager, our GM and coaches, we all had our sleeves rolled up.

There were more directors in 'Quality Winning Football' than in any other pillar. It seemed to me that quite a few of my fellow directors got a kick out of being involved with the actual football, which was understandable I guess, when the board was elected from the club's fanbase. They were very quick to share anecdotes, trivia and knowledge of football games whenever the opportunity presented itself, almost like prize birds showing each other their tail feathers, I reckoned. By contrast, of course, I had absolutely zero footballing tail feathers to parade. The board were amused that I'd even had to ask Arsenal and Netherlands forward Vivianne Miedema what her name was when she visited the Pan to watch her then girlfriend play Lewes one Sunday. She was very nice about the fact that though I'd introduced myself as a director, I didn't know the name of perhaps one of the greatest living female players at the time. I told her truthfully that I did recognise her face but just couldn't think of her name. Just as I suspect Madonna or Prince might have done, she simply offered me her hand with a warm smile and said, 'Miedema.' So cool, so graceful. I introduced her to my friend Annabella, who was watching her first women's football match, and Miedema was humbly kind and interested, obliging us with a photograph together.

So I had plenty to do with work *off* the pitch, and stayed away from the QWF pillar. However, Ed R and Maggie were particularly keen that we get a female to head up our football provision, and were in touch with Kelly Lindsey, a former player for the US Women's national team, currently working as director of football with the Moroccan women's national team and previously head coach of the Afghan women's team, where she had blown the whistle on the awful sexual abuse scandal there, exposed with the help of the *Guardian*'s Suzy Wrack. I looked Kelly up and found a powerful and emotional clip of her talking about the Afghan team on YouTube. She seemed to be an orator with a big heart, and one who knew women's football and, crucially, what it meant to be a woman playing football, inside out. She was sure enough of herself to show visible emotion when she spoke, willing to cry in front of an audience. Would someone of this calibre be interested in a move to England to work at Lewes FC?

Maggie and Ed were persuasive, and Kelly was curious about the equality project at Lewes FC, as well as being keen to explore a new culture. There was some tension on the board about exactly what it was she would be doing, but this was symptomatic of the typical everyday struggle we faced: we had expertise and experience with men's non-league football, but we were straining at the bit to progress on the women's side and establish a high-performance ethic and an academy that would feed our vision for the whole club. As pioneers, though, playing against the big guys and trading on our difference, we had little experience in this side of the game. We needed support to transition to a more professional environment, and those of us who recognised the lack of knowledge and shared the vision of progression knew we needed Kelly. And amazingly, we got her!

Kelly joining Lewes FC had a profound effect on both my understanding of football and my self-confidence within football, and I'll be for ever grateful to her for that.

When she first came to Lewes, she was an ingénue in terms of men's football culture, having never attended a British men's football match, non-league or otherwise. She seemed a genuine person who wanted to elevate others and was at home with performing. With a positive mental attitude and nothing to prove, she was full of cheery greetings, sometimes breaking into song if the occasion demanded it (or even when it didn't). She was keen to understand the culture and did a lot of listening and shadowing. Eventually she got stuck into the women's side, and then tried to get just as involved on the men's, but that was trickier for all sorts of reasons. However, she rarely complained (unless it was about 'the crap cold weather').

Kelly spoke to us all (me, the team, fans at the Pan) about how lucky we were to have our passports. How privileged we were, as women, to be playing and watching football freely as we chose to. The women in Afghanistan, she explained, played football just to show other women that there was another way of being than having to stay cooped up at home in service, only allowed out at the discretion of male members of their families. She made me see that Lewes FC's actions were important to women in far-flung corners of the globe, women who were denied anything *like* equal pay. We were all aware that football spoke to men all around the world, and that news about the club had reached almost 40 different countries (we knew this because our owners now spanned that many countries; I recall the virtual Slack cheer when we checked Fiji off the list!). Kelly brought home the fact that there were women in so many countries who had little freedom in their lives, and who were treated as second-class citizens in every way we could imagine. For those women, knowing that somewhere in the world there were women who were actually paid the same as their male counterparts to play *football* – well, that was 'a frigging big deal'. A ray of hope and possibility. So Kelly brought a wider perspective and more value to our project. And she stayed, *always*, as she liked to put it, 'significantly insignificant'. She was behind the scenes, she watched every game, analysing, spotting patterns, she coached clearly and professionally. She didn't do too much media because she was at the training ground, but what she did do, she absolutely smashed.

My first experience of Kelly's coaching (i.e., simply how she was as a person) was after I'd done a short talk in the Rook Inn for players. As I left the front of the room and walked to the back, she looked me straight in the eye, put her hand up for a high five and said warmly, 'Really well done – you smashed it.' I loved this new, encouraging culture, where I felt part of a bigger picture, part of a team.

We went on to do talks together, for SisterShips groups, for the police, at conferences, and became friends, even going on holiday together. I learned a lot. Firstly, I came to understand more about the differences in development between men's and women's football, and the sheer amount of catching up in both confidence and style the women have in front of them. Kelly told me that on the coaching and performance side, a lot of the staff in women's football at this level are not experienced, despite the elite league the women play in. Coaches are 'straight outa uni and doing things out of a book. We need to sort this,' she said. We needed to upskill our young athletes too, bringing in more psychology, more nutrition, more life skills. 'How do you eat?

How do you take care of yourself? How do you handle stress? These are important questions for these young women,' she said.

I asked lots of my own questions. Kelly called me 'K Dobs', or 'the K-Dawg', drawing me into the football gang with a nickname and explaining in plain and human terms that every woman plays football for a reason. 'Maybe they didn't start as little girls with any reason,' she explained, 'but by the time they are teenagers, there is a good reason why they still play.'

We talked about the importance of values and leadership, and developing a human-centred environment at the Pan. I could relate to her coaching ideas via my experiences in counselling – working out how to deeply respect people and understand their unpredictability, how to cut them slack for the vicissitudes we are always experiencing in life, and how important it was to provide the right kind of environment to facilitate change. Having had many surgeries herself, Kelly was very concerned about the inferior medical care offered to female athletes, and we met sports medicine specialist Dr Eva Carneiro together for advice. Eva – herself affected by sexist media reporting around her time as a doctor for Chelsea's men's team[24] – had become an owner

24 Dr Carneiro had formerly been the team doctor for Chelsea's men's team. She brought a case of constructive dismissal and discrimination against the club in 2016 following an incident in 2015, when she went onto the pitch to help an injured player, fulfilling her professional duty in line with medical ethics and safety protocols. This had appeared to anger then manager José Mourinho. Following the incident, Dr Carneiro complained that she was subjected to intense media scrutiny, including sexist commentary. She also said she received abusive

at Lewes because of the Call Him Out campaign and was very supportive, on hand to help when we needed it.

Speaking at events with Kelly was a total vibe. I'll never forget a corporate event she, Charlie, Maggie and I were invited to, where we spoke one afternoon about how to find your purpose in life, and how it might align with your work, and Kelly told the assembled audience that they should wake up every morning, look at themselves in the mirror and shout, 'I am a champion!' We stayed overnight and had breakfast with the employees the next morning. As the company CEO arrived, everyone stood up, much to her surprise, and shouted, 'I am a champion!' It was very loud, very funny, and it brought tears to our eyes.

As time ticked on, more females were elected or co-opted to the Lewes board. During my last year, if we included senior leadership too, we temporarily achieved a 50/50 gender mix across management and directors – a real milestone – though sadly it wasn't to last long, and I never lost my sense of not quite fitting in on the board.

What is it, though, that marks someone out as an outsider in any given environment? This is a question that really matters, for two reasons. Firstly, because defining yourself as an imposter means that you can identify where you can make the biggest

---

messages online, including threats and misogynistic remarks. Dr Carneiro left the club later that year, having been demoted. The case was settled out of court, reportedly for a significant financial sum, and the club apologised unreservedly to Dr Carneiro. It highlighted the challenges faced by women working in non-footballing roles within the men's game.

difference in an organisation. This may seem counterintuitive, as the regular wisdom says that people add most value in an area where they have the most experience and expertise. I understand of course that there will be plenty of professions where this holds true. You don't want your doctor to be unqualified, and no one feels comfortable with an amateur airline pilot. However, in organisations that are essentially based on understanding customers (and colleagues) as whole people, with a myriad of motivations and needs, the outsider is your secret weapon. They are the person who is fine asking 'dumb' questions. They challenge, quite possibly unwittingly, the orthodoxy of *we've-always-done-it-like-that* or *people-won't-like-that*.

The second reason why outsider-spotting is so important is to do with how, or rather *whether*, they are supported by the non-outsiders, that is, the *in*siders who surround them. I know this from first hand. I initially thought that what marked me out as an outsider in football was bound to be my sex. Football is dominated from boardroom to terraces by men. (Assume, for the sake of brevity, that I've given you countless examples and heaps of data to support this statement, because, well, you and I both know it's true.) But, breaking news, my own experience led me to a more nuanced understanding of the outsider. There is an even more powerful defining characteristic than whether you are male or female, even on hyper-male Planet Football. That characteristic is 'belonging'. This means that not all women in football wholly welcomed my presence in their industry. So this next passage was one of the hardest to write, because it brought back what were some of my most unexpected and hardest moments in Lewes FC.

Coach Kelly's inclusive and effusive attitude was particularly important for me, because it was at times, like Shannon's and Roodie's before her, a lifeline. There were other female allies too. But I'll be honest, there were some upsetting episodes where some 'sisters' kind of . . . left me out. It was never intentional, I'm sure, but the effect was nonetheless hurtful. The women most likely to exclude me were those who had serious credentials in sport or business, or both. I started with credentials in neither, it's true. It was an observable truth that my not following the rules of sport and commerce (because I didn't know them) enabled countless conversations and connections. No one had told me you don't just email the chief executive of Virgin Active or Unilever. But I did. And they replied personally, and several opportunities were opened up by that. No one told me that a football match is not the place to host 'political' speeches, so, as mentioned, I approached Helen Pankhurst to give a talk on women's rights on the terraces before the women's team's big match versus Manchester United.

I think that perhaps some of those women who had worked so hard to attain a voice and credibility within football were, unconsciously, wary of their association with the complete nutter who didn't even know who Vivianne Miedema was. But knowing how incredibly hard a woman has to work to become accepted in football, part of me understands that expending some of that 'acceptance capital' on introducing the female outsider to other experienced insiders was a big ask. Again, I think these were likely to have been in-the-moment, unconscious choices. But it has taken me some time to, as they say in modern parlance, 'unpack that'.

Even while on the board, there were multiple times I felt left out of invitations to attend sports-related celebratory events by other women, or times when I'd be at an event and felt I needed to work hard to get women I knew to introduce me to people. Once, for example, I was in a Zoom meeting with a group of senior leadership, and at the end of the call, the other females in the group agreed a meeting place for an event that evening. I asked where they were going. They explained they had free tickets to a glamorous-sounding launch of a sports initiative and at this point I felt things became a little uncomfortable. These women had strong sports sector backgrounds, and they were going with other female staff at Lewes FC, but I hadn't been invited. Awks. There were similar occasions. I got used to it, almost. But I did feel hurt and disappointed sometimes, believing I wasn't getting to join in the fun with them (left on the bench, I guess!), and I remember having to work on my own feelings about incidents like these in order not to let them affect the spirit I needed for my work.

I think there are brilliant skills one learns from team sport, but as I've said in a previous chapter, I didn't get to play much of that growing up. However, resilience and leadership, two good examples of what sports participation can teach, are qualities that being an outsider did require me to learn for myself, and fast. My learning was definitely accelerated and enhanced by my decades-long practice of Buddhism. That brought out the ability for self-reflection and introduced me to the powerful concept of 'turning poison into medicine'. In other words, using difficulties as springboards for growth. Buddhism taught me to use the experience of exclusion as a valuable lesson in prioritising *inclusion* as a leader. When you know how something feels, you can be doubly inspired not to let anyone else feel like that.

However, I'd still say to any organisation employing the kind of people who don't currently exist in your power structures or conform to your cultural norms, 'Take those people outside your building' – i.e., use them externally as well as internally. Be confident in your differentiating edges if you really want to leverage equality and diversity. They will ask questions that everyone else who 'went native' years ago wouldn't think to ask, or, more likely, wouldn't *dare* to ask, for risk of exposing themselves as not knowing everything.

Chapter 21
The Rooker Prize

———

Some things are too important to be taken seriously.

Oscar Wilde

In 2021, we had a Christmas party. We were all relieved that we could do this after the various lockdowns, the endless COVID testing of players and staff, the behind-closed-doors matches and the mask-wearing. A merry group of directors, staff, volunteers and players, from the women's and men's teams, gathered in fancy dress in a venue close to the Pan. We enjoyed a mince pie, a drink and a laugh – it was great fun to see everyone outside of their normal kit (literally and figuratively) – and we danced, sang, took the mickey and, in my case, chatted away with support staff about how we were all thwarted writers.

Biram was sure he had a sci-fi novel in him but didn't have the time to write it. Clive, former director, current minibus driver and kit man on the men's side, reckoned he could give us all a run for our money with some great romantic fiction but was also too busy with his multitude of duties. Amanda, safeguarding officer, said she had a great idea for a real-life story, and we were all aware that Shrey, our fan and community engagement manager, fancied himself as a poet. Ed Ramsden was another who believed he could write a novel if only he had some free time. Charlie suggested they all pen their pieces and we'd judge who was the best. This quickly developed into the idea of holding a writing competition for Rooks owners where they'd only have to come up with the first 250 words – that way no one would have an excuse. In a burst of inspiration, I declared that it would be called the Rooker Prize – a competition to rival the famous Booker and finally, cheekily, cement our status as a club leading the way in the arts (not that we were trying to do this exactly, but what with posters, statues and the odd art exhibition, we *were* inadvertently getting there). Charlie said he'd put forward a prize of £250 to the winner to donate to their chosen charity, and I appointed myself head judge, because I'd thought of the name and that is how it works after a glass of wine.

Post-Christmas I was busy and quite willing to let the idea slip – just one of those things you say at a party that you're never going to action. However, Biram emailed to ask when I was getting it off the ground, as he'd written his 250 words and was encouraging Ed to do the same. Clive was keen too, apparently, and nurturing a bodice-buster as we spoke. So, obligingly, I looked up some dates and found that 27 April is International Crow and Raven Appreciation Day (ICRAD). Who knew? This was surely a day all Rooks fans should observe? The universe was talking, and I decided that we'd run the Rooker and announce a winner on 27 April. You see, at this stage in my outsider's journey, I might have become a little tempted to assimilate and fit in – to pretend I was a normal football club director, who thought a lot about football and not so much about odd things like, I don't know, literary competitions named after corvids that poke fun at the establishment. But then I might have lost my outsider superpower, and the club needed to keep the attention of all those owners who maybe weren't so into the football but loved the message of change. My allies were keen, so I thought, 'Better get on with it.'

I asked two proper writers (and club owners, of course) – women's football journalist and author Suzy Wrack, and my friend Mark Crick, who is a photographer as well as an author – to join me on a judging panel, and hastily established some criteria. We then invited all Lewes owners to enter. I set the closing date specifically to give us time to judge the entries and announce the result on ICRAD, and enjoyed writing a press release to encourage people to become owners of Lewes FC just so that they could take part in this new and exclusive literary competition. I tried introducing myself to people as 'head judge of the Rooker Prize', hoping that they'd ask me what on earth I was talking about. My friend Neil, whittler extraordinaire, who makes effigies every year for Bonfire, came round for dinner. I told him about the Rooker. A week later, he surprised me with an awesome hand-carved trophy shaped like a pen nib and fashioned from a piece of my old oak banister, given to him years ago. It had 'The Rooker Prize' carved on it in brass and was a splendid thing. Biram was very happy.

We took the judging most seriously. Charlie separated the pieces from their cover emails for me, anonymising them so that there could be no bias. We read the entries separately, making notes, and then convened for lunch, discussing our thoughts and responses. The inaugural Rooker Prize was won by Duncan Brown, who wowed us with 'Black Premonition', a Gothic piece involving crows and a dripping pan, which he said he really enjoyed writing. 'Quite a change from my day job as a medieval archaeologist,' he laughed.

When I eventually left the board, it was agreed I'd keep the Rooker going, and so the following year, I started looking for sponsorship. I remember bumping into a pal from the terraces, John Briley, in the garage while waiting for my wing mirror to be fixed, and chatting to him about getting sponsors to cover the prize money, a reproduction trophy for the winner and the judging lunch. John put me in touch with another Lewes fan, Tarquin, who produces a podcast called *The Rockonteurs*, in which Gary Kemp (Spandau Ballet) and Guy Pratt (Pink Floyd) converse with music legends and share stories. Guy had moved nearby and popped into the Dripping Pan for a cuppa. They were happy to sponsor us, and what's more, Guy's wife, Georgia Byng – a popular children's author – was up for joining the judging panel.

Meanwhile, I contacted Hachette UK, a leading publishing house, whose website said that they 'value different and diverse perspectives, voices and ideas to support creativity and break new ground', and that they had 'a hunger to learn, to take on unfamiliar ideas and activities and to explore new experiences'. I very much liked the sound of these statements, and sure enough, they agreed to offer the winner an hour with a specialist editor at their London HQ to help them on their way to finishing their story.

So with two excellent sponsors and another judge, the Rooker Prize ran for a second year, once again attracting diverse and fun entries. Ronnie Hendra, a science teacher from London who had recently become an owner of the club after the women's Euros and hearing an interview with CEO Maggie, won the competition with 'The Teeny Tiny Toaster Dragon'. It was an ingenious opener, and Guy Pratt presented her with the trophy at a Lewes women's match. I was invited to Hachette UK's London HQ with Ronnie for a tour, before she was taken in for her hour with an editor.

Just another example of an idea that likely wouldn't have happened in another football club. We were growing a culture where we could have a joke, then run with it. 'If you create a culture where traditionally marginalised people feel safe, welcome and valued, they feel confident enough to express themselves and then give more in terms of creativity and discretionary effort,' as diversity and inclusion consultant (and my good friend) David Hare says. And these were the things – the Rooker, Brad's Pit, the beach huts, Prosecco on tap, the pirate statue, the breastfeeding area – that we always ended up talking about to potential sponsors, at conferences, and to visiting companies at our awayday workshop sessions. People are engaged by the stuff that is challengingly different, and those crazy, unlikely things can be the very ones that will help the organisation grow and may well change the story.

Postscript: As I send this book to my publishers, I'm delighted to share that Lewes FC owner, Baroness Lola Young (remember her from the APPG Shannon and I attended?) popped down to Lewes for a visit. As I showed her around the Pan, she surprised me by offering to Chair the Rooker Prize, mentioning that she had previously chaired the actual Booker. Her exact words were, 'Karen, wouldn't it be great to become the only person to have chaired the Booker and the Rooker?' I smiled very widely – because it really is great!

Chapter 22
A Witch's Portal

Men: Football's coming home!! It's coming home! It's coming!!
Women, 60 years later: FFS, I'll get it myself!
Amy Wright, English teacher and mum, on Twitter/X

During the summer of 2022, England's Lionesses achieved
something the men's team hadn't managed since 1966: they won
an international competition. The Euros was held in England,
with matches taking place around the country, including at nearby
Brighton's Amex stadium. It was a heady couple of months for
anyone involved in women's football. The Lionesses were on
billboards, front covers, TV screens and social media feeds. And
with record-breaking numbers, both at stadiums and for TV
audiences, it seemed like the whole country was behind England's
women's team. TikTok videos of female footballers went viral as
members of the team suddenly became household names.

'Nationalism trumps sexism,' remarked Kelly wryly as the
women's game in England became indisputably popular.

As a result, we witnessed clubs paying more attention to, and putting more investment into, their women's sides to compete in the increasingly professional domestic leagues. The Euros had proven what we at Lewes FC had been railing about – and banking on – for years: that there was indeed both a live and a TV market for women's football.

It felt like every podcast I listened to, every interview I was invited to do, every news story I read about women's football hyped the fact that investors, clubs, sponsors and broadcasters were poised to throw all their money at female football teams. What was the reality, though? Was feminism in action really about to take over the world? And were there potential dangers to watch out for?

The truth was that despite earning more in sponsorship revenue than other Championship and many Women's Super League teams, we at Lewes FC had to work very hard to hit our financial targets. One difficult issue was that most potential sponsors looked at social media impressions (i.e., the number of engaged fans seeing posts that mentioned or showed them), rather than the quality of the narrative, or the ability to springboard us via a meaningful partnership and help co-create that narrative. Having made history, and broken new ground, we at Lewes were open to exploring and defining new ways forward, but unfortunately (and unimaginatively), impressions, website traffic, the amount of media coverage and the number of social media followers were the ways that sponsors traditionally quantified their output in (men's) football, and we needed to attract funds from groups who understood that *women's* football was a very different offering, and that 'success' in this arena might therefore be measured in a different way. We needed to help them see football through the female-influenced lens of the women's game.

Both games might be called 'football', but to many fans, they held distinctly different meanings, carrying distinctly different messages. We knew that new fans of the women's game were currently more likely to buy merch and to display 'brand loyalty' to any sponsor supporting women's football. We knew they were equally as likely to follow a player to a different club than stick to a club once the player they admired had left. We knew they were more familiar with tech and online communities, more purpose-led and values-driven, and less likely to watch football on TV on a weekend afternoon or evening (the favoured way of many male fans). We posited that the success of women's football sponsorship could instead be measured by how it affected the physical, mental and emotional well-being of those it engaged with, including the value to the world of promoting gender equality. I'm talking about depth rather than breadth.

Women's football's growing popularity and professional development meant there was now particular pressure on us to bring in revenue faster, because other, much bigger clubs in our league could lean into their men's resources to better accommodate their nascently popular women. To give the situation context, Lewes FC's turnover in the 2021–2 season was approximately £1.5 million. The women's and men's playing budgets were around £250,000 each for the whole season. For the women to stay in the second tier, Lewes had to adhere to ever-increasing licence requirements (number of support staff, number of turnstiles, player contact hours, standard of floodlights, etc.). And due to our comparative lack of human and financial resources, it was clear that we were as yet unable to properly test our financial model of mass ownership, which, marketed well, had the potential to reach enough owners to propel Lewes forward to the hallowed Super League. We might not have had a rich men's side, but we had the potential power of a collective that would believe in our mission. Every 14,000 owners would make us £1,000,000 in revenue. Oh, for the time and money to activate them!

So effectively we were in a race against time to bring money in, and without dismantling the entire patriarchal football system first, we were on track to lose. We'd worked too hard and come too far to go without a fight, so I was about to have one last go at bringing some more money in quickly – via investment.

I got on a plane with Coach Kelly and we flew to the obvious place for a football club needing investment in its women – the City of the Goddess. We were off to attend the Athens Women's Football Summit, alongside my Lewes co-director Lucy Mills – an expert on both Web 3.0[25] and women's football – who was

---

25 Web 3.0 describes the next phase of the internet, focusing on decentralisation, blockchain technology and user empowerment. Similarly, women's football emphasises empowerment and decentralisation by breaking traditional barriers and gaining autonomy in a male-dominated sport. You could say that both Web 3.0 and women's football reshape established systems and promote greater equity and inclusion.

doing important work on the club's connections with our owners around the world. This was to be a significant event for me because it inadvertently ended up connecting me closely to Lewes FC – accidentally of course – for another year.

The Athens Women's Football Summit is a gathering of stakeholders in the women's football industry worldwide, taking place in the city that introduced democracy to the world. Set up by New York-based human rights lawyer Marios Christos Sfantos, the annual conference brings together top business, investment, broadcasting, NGO, governmental and sporting stakeholders for 'two days of powerful discussions and presentations'. During the worldwide lockdown of 2020, I had spoken alongside Charlie, our then goalkeeper Tatiana 'Safe Hands' Saunders, and the feminist activist Gill Whitty-Collins (author of the excellent *Why Men Win At Work*) at the summit's second year on Zoom. President Marios, mentioned above, is a smartly suited and charming self-confessed anarchist, passionate about both women's football and connecting people in the industry. He had linked with Lewes FC as a 'strategic partner' for his summit because of our equality messaging. Over communal glasses of wine on Zoom with various high-profile international stakeholders in women's football, he described the summit as an industry-leading international gathering, and with his aligned views on the social purpose of the women's game worldwide, he soon became a valued friend.

Over the last couple of seasons at Lewes, it was an increasingly clear and pressing priority for our board to target high-net-worth investors or big sponsorship deals that would enable Lewes FC

Women to continue playing at the level they were at, and the club to keep its platform setting a global example of doing football differently and treating players fairly and respectfully, while campaigning for and demonstrating change in the game. While we had brought the club to a certain level, with the women in the Championship, improved facilities, a more professional staff and an award-winning culture, we were painfully aware that without the big bucks of Premier League-associated women's sides, we were in danger of losing our Championship platform. If we were to lose our place in the Championship, we would lose league-associated grants and rights monies, but also women's football *itself* would lose out in this crucial stage of its development, on a club like ours bringing its independent ideas and influence to the elite-level decision-making boards. Currently Maggie occupied Lewes FC's place on those boards, which would determine the future of English women's football. We were acutely aware that our voice was perhaps the only one completely free of the influence of big men's clubs. If women's football wanted to stay true to its values, and not become a spare rib to the men's game, we needed the money that would keep us in the Championship.

Marios had asked me to come over to Athens in 2022, describing the annual event as 'a unique investment, business collaboration, policy development, networking, educational and innovational focal point'. But I saw it in much simpler terms: a few days making friends with like-minded folk and a last-ditch attempt to find investment for Lewes FC Women (and therefore freeing up resources for the whole club). I was eager to get off

Zoom and attend in person, and looking forward to a few days in the Greek sunshine with high-powered people who might be willing to work with the best club in the world. Kelly and Lucy were my allies: women with an exhaustive knowledge of football, but who saw the power of letting me be myself within it. We were all on the same page, and after the experience of various board obstacles, it was a relief.

Kelly and I flew from the grey of the UK to sunny Athens, meeting Lucy there (at that point she worked for FC Barcelona as well as being on the Lewes board). Over beers in an outdoor restaurant, we planned our 45-minute presentation knowing we could knock socks off with our tale of disruption. I would introduce the club, its ownership model, Equality FC and our values and vision; Lucy would talk specifically about our owners worldwide, giving statistics and encouraging every delegate to sign up as an owner; and Kelly, well, she would be Kelly – the ultimate orator. We simply had to unleash her on the stage!

The day before our talk, Kelly and I visited Athena's temple – the Parthenon at the Acropolis. Inspired, I decided to open my address to the delegates with a nod to Ares and Athena. (Stick to football? Not me!) These two children of Zeus couldn't have been more different in personality. Ares was the hot-headed, bloodthirsty and brutal god of war and courage. Athena, goddess of wisdom and military victory, was patron of our host city. She was famous for strategic vision, a cool head and tactical thinking, and, accordingly, she was often depicted with a helmet and a shield, and carrying a wise owl on her shoulder. These two gods reminded me of some of the qualities that had been taken on by men's football over the years versus the developing ones of the women's game. I well remembered people telling me that the women's game was more technical because the female players lacked the strength and pace of their male counterparts but were more thoughtful – hello, Athena! I considered the trajectory of the men's game, and all the money, power and egos involved in it globally, as well as the away men's matches I had attended over the last few years where segments of the crowd seemed a little too edgy, chants a little too nasty. And then I thought about the women's game, and how comparatively *free* it currently was – wiser, friendlier, less dramatic, more strategic, reflective even. If only grandstanding Ares would learn from practical Athena and not the other way around. Of course, England's Lionesses had just won the Euros in England, and the atmosphere at the stadiums had been joyful, effervescent, peaceful, while the crowds had been far more diverse than those I'd seen at men's matches. I'd even attended a match alone at the Amex in Brighton, using public transport to get back and forth at night. I'd never felt safer. These crowds consisted of families, groups of young women, groups of young men, older people, women wearing headscarves, and there were smiles everywhere I looked.

So, sporting my Athena T-shirt purchased in a gift shop near the Parthenon the day before, I opened our talk by publicly thanking the Athens Women's Football Summit for having us, while paying tribute to the city, its namesake and women's football, and then sharing my Ares and Athena analogies. And of course, I told the business and sport delegates about the little club on the south coast of England that was hell-bent on changing the world through football, citing my own change of heart around the game too, just five years back, as a new Customer Zero. Lucy then took to the stage to explain about our owners and the extensive work she'd done surveying them. And lastly, Kelly blew them all away imploring them to be authentic – just like Lewes FC! – and telling them why and how to bring their whole selves to work.

During the summit, we made some heart-to-heart connections, and were particularly impressed by one entrepreneur who was keen to combine the women's game with entertainment and had clearly put his money where his mouth was. John Reynal had created an international competition called the Women's Cup, and built and dismantled a whole stadium in a few days just to host it. Plucking up courage, we invited him and his girlfriend for cocktails, and joined them at their hotel in the late afternoon on our final day. Our conversation grew into a long dinner, and so it was that I found myself, past midnight, sitting at a table in the grand dining room of a fancy hotel in the Athens Riviera, enjoying a three-course meal. Opposite me was Kelly, international coach extraordinaire; beside me was entrepreneur John, who'd been relating the story of when he tried to outbid David Beckham for Inter Miami's stadium site; and along the table were Alesandro from Microsoft; fellow Lewes director Lucy, resident of Barcelona; Shon, Kenyan football presenter; and Selva, Argentinian model, trainee accountant and John's girlfriend.

Marios, the summit founder, would join us later, but meanwhile I was telling a story that had little to do with football. It was a true story about my black Labrador, Padmé, who at one point had refused to go into our front room for some weeks and acted quite depressed. After fruitless visits to a number of vets, it transpired that she was 'affected by unseen energies from the network of Sussex churches' (according to a Lewes alternative practitioner). This revelation followed an unlikely series of events that included, variously, an animal whisperer, a white witch, a divine portal, the discovery of karmic knots, and me pretending to fetch sticks during our daily walks in order to sell the experience of being a dog to Padmé, who, according to the whisperer, may have been under the illusion that she was still a Chinese warrior from a previous lifetime. Listen, it was complicated. And got weirder by the minute. But I was in full-disclosure mode with my illustrious, if somewhat bemused, football dinner partners. Each stage of the story was interrupted by either waiters or the need for John to translate the tale into Spanish so that Selva would understand. I wasn't sure there was a language barrier as such, given the unusual nature of the yarn, but both John and Lucy were fluent Spanish speakers and seemed to be really enjoying the task: '*Sí, una bruja le habló al perro.*'

By the time I got to the point where my 12-year-old son and his friends came in from school to hear huffing and puffing in the front room, the whole table was giggling. 'What's that noise?' asked my son. And of course, I'd gamely explained, because there was really nothing else for it but the truth, that there was a witch in the lounge creating a divine portal for negative energy to travel through, and that she was possibly getting a bit out of breath.

The boys looked entirely unsurprised, and went out into the back garden to play football. Eventually the witch came out of the living room. She looked like she had been hit by a bus – dishevelled hair, confused eyes. Exhausted, she reported, 'I started to create the portal, but it got so big, I realised it was attracting all of the negative energy in Sussex!' No wonder she was tired. And frankly, I was a bit worried about the front room carpet. Overwhelmed by the magnitude of the portal, she left, promising to return the following week, and eventually finished the job by emailing a wizard in Boston, as you might when it all gets a bit much. (If you want more on this, it's for another book.)

It was a long story, with unexpected twists and turns. I enjoyed telling it at this impromptu dinner because I was effectively opening up to new friends about life in Lewes, about myself, showing a receptiveness to different ideas, demonstrating the ability to form a narrative – and also, simply, because I loved my dog very much. I should say that my embarking on this supernatural story was not random; I was prompted to tell it because John had casually mentioned earlier that he had snapped up 60 acres in Patagonia and was building a house there, but that the contractors working on the house couldn't sleep at night due to light from a UFO. I felt like my own energy story would help him feel connected and at home with us. I couldn't conjure up a more disarming image than the one of me, apparently with 'a spot of non-existence in my spine connected to deep terror from aeons ago', throwing a stick for myself by the River Ouse in Lewes so that the dog could watch me enthusiastically galumph after it and bring it proudly back to her. I was trying to cure us both, following the witch's instructions (of *course* I was), but to be honest, wouldn't you just know it, the dog was more interested in sniffing the reeds around the river than anything I was embarrassing myself doing.

We heard other stories during the course of the evening. Everyone was now opening up! And finally (was it 2 a.m.?), we talked enthusiastically about the need for funding in women's football, and its great potential as a very different product to the men's game. We spoke of the technological literacy of its fans, the communities (both physical and online) that might be created through it, the idea of combining women's matches with music concerts. I think it was when John asked me how far London was from Lewes and whether fans might travel from there to go to an event at the Dripping Pan that I felt he might be interested in partnering with us. Trust had been created, through friendship and a joint ambition. Kelly made clear her extensive international knowledge of women's football, and her concerns and recommendations, lending authority to the creativity. John engaged with her vision for working with players in a human-centred way and nurturing authenticity. We discussed the idea of a fashion show at the Pan. We'd empower the players with strong struts and poses, partner with designers and light up the ground. Selva would teach the footballers to 'walk' and create tableaux for photo ops. In return, we would teach her English ('with a British accent' – apparently much coveted!). John would fund it as a collaborative venture with his

Women's Cup organisation. It would be fab, and a toe-dip in the water of a partnership.

And how did we get to 3 a.m. in Athens talking woo-woo shit and women's football, and planning an all-singing, all-dancing international partnership? Via the power of the outsider.

Chapter 23
They Think It's All Over

—————

'I'm not dead yet!'

Monty Python and the Holy Grail

'He's not here just to hold my handbag, you know. He's a world-class poker player, reading your faces to see if I can trust you.' So declares Victoire Cogevina Reynal to a small group of Lewes FC leadership assembled around a meeting table at a local venue. It's July 2023. I look at my colleagues' reactions to this comment (stunned, maybe gobsmacked), and can't suppress a giggle. Cogevina Reynal is John Reynal's niece and the businesswoman founder of a multimillion-dollar global investment consortium. She is both very glamorous and very pregnant, and is referring to her husband, Phil, who is indeed an internationally renowned poker player. The couple joined us earlier that day for a tour of the Dripping Pan and so that I could introduce Victoire to Maggie, Kelly and Trevor from the board. My giggle is partly a release of tension, partly genuine amusement – the drama's so high here we could be on a movie set without cameras! But then I guess international investments in world-famous football clubs are the stuff some movies might be made of; and Victoire definitely has main character energy! I'm now hoping my amusement won't indicate that either I'm not taking this seriously *or* I'm a not-to-be-trusted scallywag! But how on earth did we all get here, being lie-detected by a celebrated poker champion in a designer baseball cap?

By October 2022, I'd decided not to stand for re-election to the board at the end of my three-year term. I'd had enough of the strain of trying to be myself in a sometimes difficult environment. Rules had dictated that both Charlie and Ed step down in July 2022, having reached the end of their four-term (twelve-year) limits. They were both relieved overall: twelve years of your life, being responsible custodians and giving the club so much of your available headspace, is a pretty long stretch. While I knew that their stepping away might be a blow to the club in terms of the founder mentality and leadership they had brought to the table, on a personal level it would mean a significant reduction in support for maverick old me. Ed and Charlie were of course both themselves mavericks, and therefore natural 'outsider allies', if you like, and I now reckon that every company striving for innovation in a competitive marketplace needs those. As a double outsider, I'd often felt only just able to be effective, and to comfortably concentrate on feminism and fairness, even *with* their encouragement. Not many on the board seemed to really appreciate my insights and changes from a non-football point of view, or if they did, they never told me. I think they saw them as nice-to-have quirks rather than core to a strategy of both staying relevant and speaking to unwelcome women in the unique way that only Lewes had the credibility to do. I sometimes saw eye rolls when talking about my ideas for the club's Impact on the World, and sometimes went ahead with them despite, rather than because of, some of my colleagues.

All this isn't to say that I didn't get on with my fellow board members, or that they weren't great people – they were. It's just that people don't know what they don't know, and can't be forced to be interested in something they're just not that interested in. If men are to support women into boardroom positions to achieve innovation, then they need to a) want to actively support them (i.e., really see the need for more women on the board), and b) ask sensitive questions and really listen to the answers, then act accordingly. Women also need to actively support other women and appreciate that competency isn't the only barrier across a boardroom door: active inclusion is needed, even if the women who do the including didn't experience encouragement and support themselves on their own journey. Pioneering spirits are vital for change.

While it was true that both football and the menopause had changed me – made me more assertive, less inclined to be people-pleasingly polite, more resilient than 2017 Karen, and chock-full of friendly, albeit, let's face it, slightly self-conscious fist bumps – I knew it would be more challenging than ever without those two original allies. Truth be told, I couldn't drop the need for validation and inclusion: no woman is an island, as John Donne might have said.

And I didn't want my ways to assimilate into 'football's ways'. Yes, I loved a high five, but I was always going to draw the line at using the term 'at the end of the day' after each match, for example, or walking on the pitch to speak to the manager as if I owned the place. I couldn't use a football cliché and feel genuine, and I wouldn't have been able to spontaneously put a foot on the hallowed turf for fear of overstepping my authority. Despite being a nonconformist football club director, as a woman, I still felt a strong attachment to my lifelong sculpting. As American writer Audre Lorde famously said, 'It's not our differences that divide us, it's our inability to recognise, accept, and celebrate those differences.' Crucially, there on the board, my difference had also been my purpose. And I knew it wasn't universally understood or celebrated.

To add to all this, I was sleeping irregularly (thank you, age-related hormonal changes), had some health issues I couldn't ignore, and found it hard to keep boundaries around the amount of club work I took on. When you lead on an area called 'Impact on the World', the possibilities are both excitingly limitless and demandingly so. It's hard to chill. What's more, despite employing more staff, none of the new employees were operating on the Impact on the World goals. This left me in charge of, and activating on . . . everything: monitoring progress, convening meetings, creating strategic partnerships and collaborating with staff to ensure representation at events, activities and campaigns – all with zero budget allocated to my pillar. I was mentally overworked and under-resourced. I needed more self-belief, better boundaries, more allyship and more hours in the day if I was to stay on the board *and* stay effective and healthy. Nurturing and activating with the SisterShips alone could be a full-time job. As an outsider, I guess you have to know when enough's enough, and the conditions for your space invasion are getting harsher. I let myself off the hook. Stepping down in November 2022, I attended my last AGM and online owners' town hall as a director, leaving position four months after Charlie and Ed. And I was beginning to wonder what I had really achieved.

Around the time I left the board, new staff joined to help with fan and community engagement, communications and commercial, all funded by the FA due to our women's team's league status and our sponsors Xero. The fashion show idea, which Lucy, Kelly and I had magicked up in Athens with John Reynal and Selva in mind, wasn't supported by senior management back at the club, and so was left dormant. Maggie went with Kelly to the US to meet with potential investors – including John – but sadly, little came of those meetings. Also sadly, Kelly left the club in May 2023, at the end of the season, her position no longer tenable due to constrained budgets. It was really hard for a small club like Lewes, despite generating our own income from sponsorship, ownership and matchday successes, to compete at this level, when other women's teams could call on their men's sides if push came to shove.

At that point, there were three other women on the board, but two resigned unexpectedly before their terms had ended, leaving just Lucy Mills and, well, middle-aged white men.

To encourage more diversity on the board, I wrote a targeted piece published by the organisation Women in Football before leaving. It appealed to women and people of marginalised backgrounds to apply for football board positions: 'Different ideas are necessary for innovation, and they are precious,' I wrote. 'Middle-aged white guys are, of course, still very welcome, but this is a direct call to people who, until now, may have felt unwelcome and not football club board material, mindful of the fact that football club boards historically have a certain composition.' That same year, Fair Game[26] reported that 'just 11.1 per cent of board members of Premier League clubs are women, dropping to 4.2 per cent in the Championship'. These statistics compared to FTSE 100[27] companies, where board members were 39.1 per cent female – the second highest of any country in the world among big public companies. So if anyone needed proof of how football lags behind in gender equality, there you are: it's even worse than in the corporate world. It's not hard to understand why.

In terms of succession, I was in touch with a young woman called Willa, who had interviewed me for a dissertation she had done in her final year at university called 'Conceptualising

---

26 Fair Game is an organisation bringing together values-driven clubs nationally to improve football governance.

27 The FTSE 100 (aka 'The Footsie') stands for the Financial Times Stock Exchange 100 index and refers to the UK's best-known stock market index of the 100 most highly capitalised blue chips listed on the London Stock Exchange. So it's fair to say, these companies are doing well.

empowerment through sport: how womxn's[28] football in the UK can be used as a tool to empower womxn and resist stereotypes'. Impressed by both that title (we could all be a bit more Gen Z) and the woman herself, I suggested she might think about writing an election address and applying for the board. So I was delighted when, at 22 years old, Willa was successful in a competitive election in which other, older candidates had not made the cut. Lewes FC's youngest ever board member would bring a youthful perspective to the club, *and* she was interested in working with the SisterShips. It was a privilege to encourage her in her work, and watch her lead on some brilliant activations with our SisterShips, but ultimately the workload, alongside a new full-time job, caused Willa to step down too, after a year.

Via my ongoing supportive relationships with Willa, and Stef McLoughlin, now head of commercial, I worried that things were looking financially bleak in 2023. Previous director donations (including my own), utilised to enable investment in key areas and make sure we broke even, were running out. I was aware that if the club didn't get money in quickly, the already lean budgets would need to be slashed, and staff would lose their jobs. Despite the laudable lack of debt – an unusual situation for a football club, and a principle we had stood by firmly as a board – Charlie and I chatted frequently at home about the increasing fragility of

---

28 The term 'womxn' is a gender-inclusive spelling of 'women', intended to be more progressive and inclusive of all gender identities. To me, it indicated that Willa would bring a Gen Z influence to our Boomer board, and make it more representative of our wider community.

the situation, especially for the women and their league status. Therefore, despite no longer being a director, I asked Maggie and the board's permission to reconnect with John Reynal in an effort to resurrect some kind of investment deal. They agreed.

Back in 2021, while still on the board, Charlie had written an internal proposal called 'Project Firework'. It concerned finding investment for the club to kick-start the women into the Super League and would bring in money in a multitude of ways. Think of the number of people who came when we'd played Manchester United in the FA Cup, or Liverpool before they got promoted. We always sold out at the Pan (capacity 2,500-ish) on these occasions. Think of the platform from which to attract new 'fans of change', and think of the sponsors who would want to align with this mouse called Lewes FC that had somehow found an independent way to roar in the highest echelons of English women's football. I often remembered Biram saying to me that getting the women into the WSL should surely be the priority, and that he wondered why the board weren't pursuing that goal, all guns blazing. I tended to agree. It made sense if we wanted to fulfil our stated mission of 'setting an example on the highest achievable platform'.

Project Firework hadn't initially gained traction inside the club. Now, however, in 2022, working in a board advisory group sct up for the purpose, Charlie had done the legal groundwork, and the board were aware that they needed more money even to stay where we were, with Maggie, Andy Gowland (newly elected director who had just joined the commercial pillar), Trevor, Lucy and Biram keen to progress and sharing Charlie's urgency.

So with hope in our hearts (we could still keep the women in the Championship and prove to the world that when you treat people fairly, *everyone* benefits), Charlie and I joined a Zoom with John, who was sitting among the ferns of a beautiful garden in Uruguay. Charlie and John spoke a similar language in terms of business, crunching numbers, outlining what a deal might look like. His interest piqued, John and girlfriend Selva then flew over to visit Lewes, and negotiations moved forward with Charlie and Andy.

I found myself cooking lunch for them in my kitchen, booking restaurants, showing Selva the Long Man of Wilmington and the beautiful Lewes Priory ruins, inviting board members over to meet the couple, even learning Spanish on Duolingo, and generally welcoming our friends from Miami. I became an 'ambassador' (the title Maggie and I agreed on to cover the relationship work I was continuing to do) while the deal was negotiated that might help the women stay in the Championship, and eventually achieve promotion.

The fact was that women's football was looking to be increasingly about who had the most money to invest in their team, and as the big clubs of the men's Premier League and Championship were slowly waking up to the earning potential of their women's sides, Lewes needed to stay on the map in a fast-growing business place. It started to feel like we'd almost been *too* successful with promoting the women's game and had shot ourselves in the foot.[29]

---

29 We knew our efforts to develop the game as a whole were helping to make the door into the WSL close more quickly.

The FIFA women's World Cup would be played in Australia and New Zealand in 2023, and with the Lionesses having won the Euros in 2022, women's football and England would once again be showcased on an international stage, and the game would only grow in popularity.

Initially the deal was progressed by Charlie and Andy, with Maggie and Trevor coming in from the board. However, after a couple of months, John became keen to involve his niece. Victoire Cogevina Reynal was at that moment planning to start the consortium Mercury 13 – named after the female astronauts who trained but never got the chance to fly, because NASA refused to allow them to be part of their official programme – and she helpfully lived in London: local compared to John in Miami. The $100 million investment group planned to buy into women's soccer (football to us, of course) teams around the world and manage them according to both business values and the values of the women's game. John's own involvement suddenly became limited as he transferred the deal to Victoire while himself becoming an investor in the Mercury 13 group. Things changed overnight.

And so, to the poker-face test. The intensity of sitting around that table, wondering if our faces were trustworthy, took the deal to a whole new level of intrigue. Reassuringly, after the meeting everyone was hugely optimistic. The mutually beneficial arrangement would inject over £5 million into the women's side of the club – so simultaneously allowing more of our budget to go to the rest of the club – and would see us move from *equality* to a more mature and appropriate position of *equity*. With this investment our women's team would be able to stay in the Championship and contest for promotion. The club would keep its staff. We would finally be able to fund a global ownership campaign that would see us reap the true and lucrative benefits of mass community ownership. Lewes FC would be set.

In order to do the deal, we would be selling 51 per cent of shares in the women's team, but important caveats in the legal documents were included, saying that Lewes FC Women would always play at the Pan, and always keep their badge and colours. And crucially, we stood to gain expertise and connections in women's football and business from the people Victoire had assembled in her consortium. Happy days.

At this point, Charlie, as he was no longer a director, was excluded from discussions and negotiations by the board, as they felt this was the right thing to do. A shame, nevertheless, because of his experience in both entrepreneurial negotiations and communications and the relationships we'd built up. With the arrival of Mercury 13, the agreement went from a more personal one involving individuals to a corporate deal bringing in many more interests. As for me, I'd finished the introductions.

Now as external fans, we watched Mercury 13 inaccurately announce that they were 'acquiring' Lewes FC Women *before* the board had communicated information about the deal to owners and took to social media to express this publicly! Some of them were naturally unhappy. Charlie and I, as engaged owners ourselves, both discussed the deal on social media. We argued that the men, and the club as a whole, would benefit from the cash injection into the women, because it would considerably relieve the central budget, and improve infrastructure, ownership revenues and sponsorship opportunities. Essentially, we called for an understanding that with the development of the women's game around us, we had outgrown equal budgets between our Championship women's team and non-league men's. We needed once again to break new ground, by demonstrating the concept of equity: giving the women's team what it needed to compete, and thereby boosting the whole club.

But some fans and owners were concerned that we would no longer be 100 per cent community-owned. Officially we still would be (via the holding company Lewes Community Football Club Limited, which in turn owned Lewes FC Women), but to all intents and purposes Mercury 13 would have a controlling interest (51 per cent of Lewes FC Women), and that sounded to some a lot like that loss of control so many Brexiteers had been afraid of. In fact, it was a way to inject resource into our women's team, with the bonus of expertise from the pool of experienced professionals Victoire seemed to be adding daily to her list of investors in the group (former Lioness Eniola Aluko, former FIFA CIO Luis Vicente, former CEO of Galatasaray and Women in Football chair Ebru Köksal). Unsurprisingly, our women players were entirely *for* the deal, as were the men's coaches and any of the men's players that I spoke to about it.

This was a stressful and trying period. The club undertook the kind of in-depth fan owner consultation that never usually happens in football. The board answered a list of over 300 questions from owners, held a virtual town hall on the subject, with Victoire answering questions too, and asked owners to vote on whether to go ahead with the investment. This meant a delay in proceedings, and time for unfounded negative comments from a small but vocal minority of fans (mainly, if not exclusively, of Lewes FC Men) on social media, which Victoire was later to tell us were discouraging.

In the end, 68 per cent of owners voted that the board *should* continue with negotiations, but the delay caused some frustration for Mercury 13. Lewes FC's senior leadership were in turn having doubts about the fit between Mercury 13 and the club. After some weeks it became clear that things were not progressing, and at the end of November 2023, investment partnership conversations were discontinued. A real shame for all involved, as with its by now strongly defined brand values, the club could have propelled any serious investor forward in its quest to advance women's football.

Following this disappointment, I felt a sense of frustration and failure. Failure because I hadn't been able to help find the money to make the equality project work to maximum effect. And frustration that I wouldn't see the club achieve its potential but might instead see the loss of the Championship platform. Gutting.

I coached myself instead to dwell on the incredible journey, the great place the club was nevertheless in, and all the victories we'd won, on and off the pitch. I remembered that our sponsors, Xero, when deciding which club to invest in, had commissioned research that found Lewes FC Women to be 'the most affinity aware' women's team in England after the Lionesses (I think that means famous!). I thought of the now many awards we'd won outside of football. I thought of the fact that 73 per cent of Lewes FC Men's supporters surveyed had said they thought about gender equality more than they did 5 years ago, and that 60 per cent of Lewes fans had undertaken a purpose-driven action inspired by the club's campaigns. I thought about how our matchday welcome was now regularly considered second to none in both leagues, and that players consistently talked of being comfortable at, and proud to play for, Lewes FC. I needed to reframe what had happened as part of the journey, and not the final destination. Kelly had encouraged me, even as an onlooker, after every match that we lost, to pick myself up, brush off the result and reframe it ('take the positives'), as they say, knowing that the fight continued. There was always the potential to rise again in the future, and, in football, it seemed, another adventure was always on its way.

I became more and more interested that season – with the Mercury 13 possibility, and the knowledge that the women's team were having their periods tracked in order to achieve a more competitive edge – in the proposition that women were 'not small men',[30] and that women's football culture shouldn't grow by default according to the example of men's. When I coincidentally met a feminist pop artist at a party that Christmas and talked to her about the club (of course!), she was keen to sponsor the women's team and help us draw attention to the specific aspects of the women's game and culture that make it

30 Thanks, Dr Stacy Sims.

different from the men's (of course!). Sadly, the women's team hadn't managed to avoid relegation – the players and CEO had left the club, leaving remaining staff to focus on rebuilding for the next season with a relatively new board. To help maintain the club's profile and values at a difficult time, I did what I was good at off the pitch, creating and managing this particular sponsorship. And so, for pre-season 2024, Charlotte Colbert's eyelashed, red-eyeshadowed open eye appeared on the front of Lewes FC Women's shirts, a portal through which to create new utopias. We erected a ten-foot-high eyelashed-eye billboard pitchside too, symbolising the invitation to view the game and the footballing environment through a female lens. To introduce Colbert's eye motif, I developed a new campaign called 'See Us As We Are', created in defiance of a system that rewards all those WSL teams financially controlled by their men's sides. And as the cause-and-effect chain surged along, Charlotte's friend, the singer-songwriter Kate Nash, wrote a song about the club and the team, featuring them in the video. The song is called 'Eyeconic'.

A wise woman advised me that once you've put your heart into something, and then you leave, 'you have to remember to take your heart back out'. Nevertheless, the clear truth is, I didn't quite manage that immediately. I think that when life presented me with the option to change the world a bit in 2017, I welcomed it wholeheartedly. After witnessing the ignorance of racism in my school years, and experiencing the way sexism had made me feel smaller and more inhibited in my own life, as well as restricting the lives of the men and women around me, here was an extraordinary chance to tangibly push things forward. Initially I'd been a little tentative, making those lists of women's organisations, going to see them, mustering the confidence to talk to them, talking to the players, while simultaneously learning about football. But then, as my confidence in Lewes FC's message built, I grabbed the opportunity firmly with both hands, developing a thirst for a fairer game, and realising changes in myself, the environment and other people's minds. Perhaps unsurprisingly, I found it hard to completely turn my back on the ongoing possibility of changing an unfair world. So, a feminist who likes a challenge, I continued for a while to act as a volunteer consultant and an ambassador for the club that dared to put its head above the parapet and choose gender equality when nobody else even saw that as a target, never mind aimed for it.

Chapter 24
Extra Time

When you stand up and demand the ball, you give others
permission to do the same.

Abby Wambach, US women's national
team player (2003–15)

It is 2023. I'm at the Dripping Pan watching Lewes v Cheshunt.
This is where I've chosen to spend my birthday afternoon. At a
men's football match, and on a cold December day too. There are
friends around me: long-term ones who've come especially to
wish me happy returns, terrace buddies I can chant and grumble
with, and praise be, even my daughter and sister are honouring
me with their attendance too. An injured striker – Ryan Gondoh –
is keeping us company, and we're talking everything from the
kombucha flavours on offer, to skincare routines, to the meaning
of life.

Around us are mainly men, with a healthy sprinkling of women
and children, and, of course, well-behaved dogs. The crowd is

passionate about what is happening on the pitch, and around me voices rise and fall as one. We all join in.

I don't feel in the slightest bit threatened standing behind the goal among the throng. I've just finished giving first-timer friends a tour of the Pan, and Fiona (first ever men's match) remarks that she's enjoying 'the warmth and friendship' shown to us here. My friend Nick smiles at the Mary Wollstonecraft quote emblazoned three feet high on a pitchside board. 'That was you, wasn't it?' he says.

It's worlds away from that alienating men's match at Wembley back in 1994.

When I first got involved in this ball game, it was to level the playing field for women. But thanks to the players, I witnessed new ways to be a woman: week in, week out, in an unfamiliar male bastion. I didn't know back then that this work would give me such a strong sense of purpose, that my issues around being excluded would surface (both on the board and in football stadiums), and more, that I'd be using my own football-bolstered, unfootbally self to trigger change in the game. I can honestly say, though, that after those few years, I now call the Dripping Pan home. And when I go to away matches – men's and women's – I no longer feel like an outsider. I'm grateful to Lewes FC for allowing me into football's inner sanctum and letting me make a mark there. Remembering how I used to feel about football, and the way it has traditionally treated my kind, I reckon this result is as great as any on the pitch.

Now it's 2024, and I'm still volunteering my time to help with the club's impact. At a women's match, I'm sipping on a rose tea from the hospitality hut (yep, diverse tea bags are setting a tone) and looking around the Pan considering what's different to the day in 2017 when I first had a cuppa here at that fateful women's game. I see the breastfeeding sign; the hoardings trumpeting equality; the beautiful hybrid grass pitch;[31] Brad's Pit with its vegetables and young fruit trees, even though Bradley has left us by now, as players do. The massive pop art female eye looks over the Pan from the south-east corner of the ground, a weird and wonderful billboard seemingly landed from an alien planet. Behind the beach huts are a line of toilets all for women, meaning there are more female toilets than men's. The lesbian pirates stand tall by the chip hut, sea buckthorn caressing their legs. I note the 'beer garden', a cordoned-off area protected from any misdirected balls and built by our Supporters' Club: it's a pitchside haven for families with small kids. Vegan offerings top the various food outlet menus. There's a much-admired flower garden by the players' steps, conjured up and nurtured by volunteer Lou. I watch fellow volunteers and stewards going out of their way to welcome everyone warmly, and then thank

---

31 Installed through grants awarded to support the growth of professionalism of teams in the FA Women's Super League and the FA Women's Championship, benefits both Lewes FC Women *and* Lewes FC Men. Previously a little bumpy and prone to a bit of flooding and freezing, it is literally a level playing field achieved through equality.

them for coming on the way out. There are a few hundred more women and girls, as well as boys and men, enjoying the match. Together we've put the 'we' right into the middle of Le-we-s, and are better off for it.

A friend from one of the SisterShips, Niamh, with a day job that involves prioritising the safety of women and girls online, is watching the match with her partner and a group of mates. She beckons me over conspiratorially, pointing at our most prolific goal-scorer. 'A little girl just told me, "I want to be like her!" ' she whispers. 'Isn't that fantastic?' She's grinning widely. 'Thanks for convincing me to give the women's game a chance,' she adds, and looks over at an older man passionately cheering nearby. 'My dad is so delighted. He could never get me to come to a football match before I heard you speak. And now I feel like part of something incredible.' Niamh's dad has been watching Lewes for nearly 60 years, and now, well, now every women's game is a chance for a family get-together.

I hope mine and Lewes' story will encourage others to make their way into areas they wouldn't normally be expected or welcome in. Because it turns out this is how we make radical change.

Recently, interviewed in front of a live audience at a business event in Brighton, I was asked, 'If you could say some words of encouragement to yourself in 2017 when you first got involved with Lewes FC, what would you say?' Quick as a flash, I knew exactly what I'd tell myself – green as I was about football then, but determined to do my bit to change the world: 'You belong. You do belong in football.'

So, if you're someone who shouldn't really be somewhere, but somehow you are . . . keep your feet under that table, be prepared to learn and give, and stay well away from the kettle. You might well be the change.

Acknowledgements

When I stepped down from the Lewes FC board towards the end of 2022, I needed therapy. As befitted the role of a custodian of this remarkable football club, I'd held many feelings –not to mention rants and ravings – inside, not wanting to inspire doubt in stakeholders or give the wrong impression. So (to save Charlie's sanity as much as my own), I found someone to offload on – a confidante to listen as I made sense of what I'd been doing for the last five or six years. I booked a few sessions with a kind and patient female counsellor, with whom I could vomit my feelings, safe in the knowledge that she was trained and paid to put up with me.

At one point during those sessions, I realised that talking wasn't quite enough – I needed to write it all down, make a book.

'Great!' said my counsellor, herself an author of therapy books. 'How long do you think it will take you?'

'A couple of weeks,' came my confident answer.

The nice woman stared.

'Just two weeks?' she asked, wobbling slightly on her chair.

'Well, OK, three,' I said. 'It'll all come tumbling out.'

So, thanks go first to Laura for the wobble and the warning glance. I realised then that I might be underestimating what's involved in writing and getting a book published. Typical.

A massive thank you to independent editor and author Susannah Waters for looking at those first outpourings with such encouraging eyes, interpreting them, and helping me shift and shape them into coherence.

Thanks too to Maura Wilding at Hachette UK for stopping me when I wouldn't shut up about Equality FC to ponder, 'Someone should really write a book about that,' and then generously putting me in touch with an editor, who put me in touch with an agent. Thank you to Nick Walters, that agent, for patiently bearing with me when I didn't understand what a book proposal was trying to do. Thanks to Trev Davies at Octopus Books for being interested, taking me on, giving such useful feedback, and coming to the Dripping Pan with his wife, Ruth, to see what all the fuss was about.

Thank you to everyone who has contributed to this book by being part of my journey with Equality FC – the Lewes FC staff, directors, coaches, volunteers, Rooks supporters (longtime and new), the journalists, the owners, the sponsors, my friends, my family, and ultimately the players. As much as football is for fans like me, it wouldn't be possible without those women and men who train during the week, build their lives around the game, and then give their all for ninety minutes at the weekend. You are endlessly inspiring (especially you women!).

Thank you Shannon Moloney, Amy Taylor, Katie Rood, Faye Baker, Jess King, Rhian Cleverly, Paula Howells, Nina Wilson, Ini Umotong, Tatiana Saunders, Georgia Robert, Bradley Pritchard, Emily Donovan, Sammy Quayle, Ellie Leek, Ella Powell, Zoe Smith, Zoe Ness, Emily Moore, Emma Thomson, Emily Kraft, Ryan Gondoh . . . and any other players I've forgotten here, who have so actively and purposefully contributed to Equality FC. Forever in your debt.

Special thanks to my friend Jamie Freeman (gone far too soon) and Donna McPhail for all the help at the beginning, and to Stef McLoughlin, Neil McLoughlin, and Boss the Dog for all the support and understanding towards the latter part of this journey.

Profound gratitude to Ed Ramsden (much as he'll hate being mentioned at all) for being cross about a once-unnoticed issue that really mattered and deciding to take a risk and do something about it.

Thanks to any family and friends who've stuck around while I became an obsessive and who still, against the odds, actually like me. Thanks to Millie and Alfie for making me laugh and being such awesome individuals and children.

Special thanks, of course, to my husband (and one-time co-director), without whom I'd no doubt be an uninspired, dry heap of reticence festering in a smelly corner somewhere, definitely not watching football. Thank you, Charlie – your love, encouragement and inspiration are constant and invaluable.

If, having read *P/Bitch Invasion*, you're inspired to support Lewes FC (and how could you not be?), please use the QR code below. You, too, can enter a world you perhaps never dreamed of and become an owner of a very special football club . . .

Index